Christmas, 1997

To our darling Grace —

I have mothered you + watched you mother your own for many years. It's been my privilege + reward, which I know you understand. We love you mightily — terrible ~~syntax~~ usage, but you get the picture.

Love,

Mom + Dad

CELEBRATIONS IN ART

MOTHERS & CHILDREN

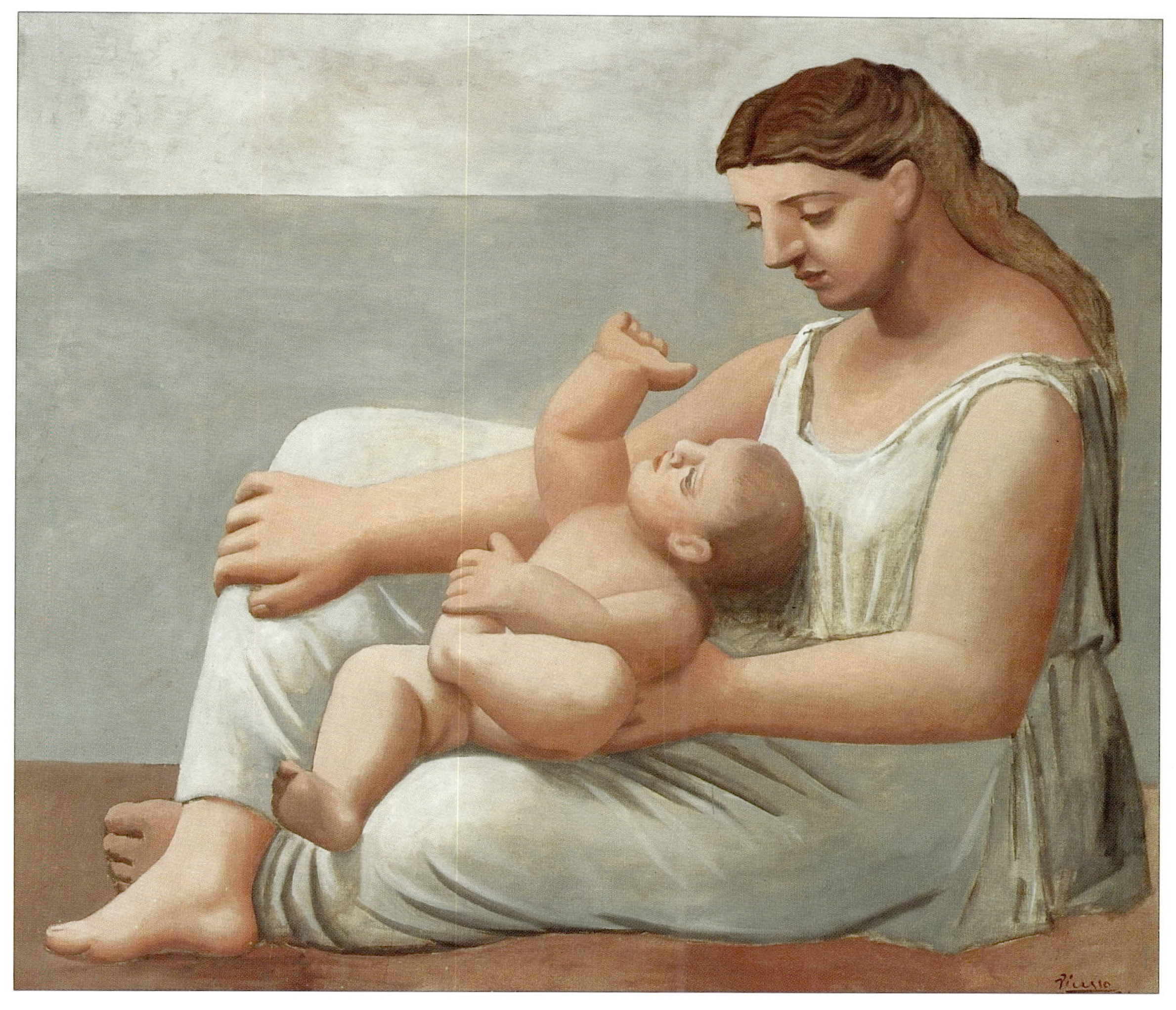

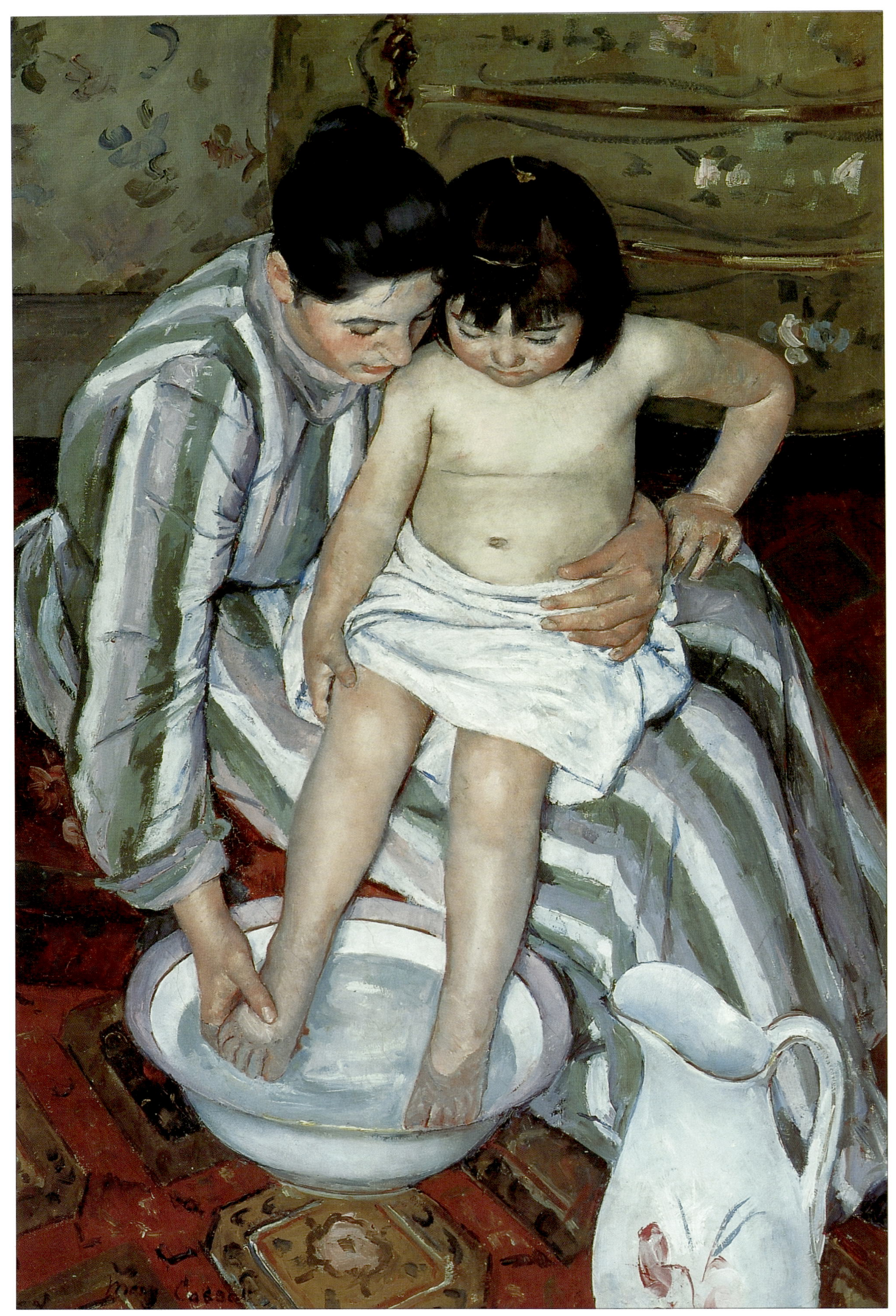

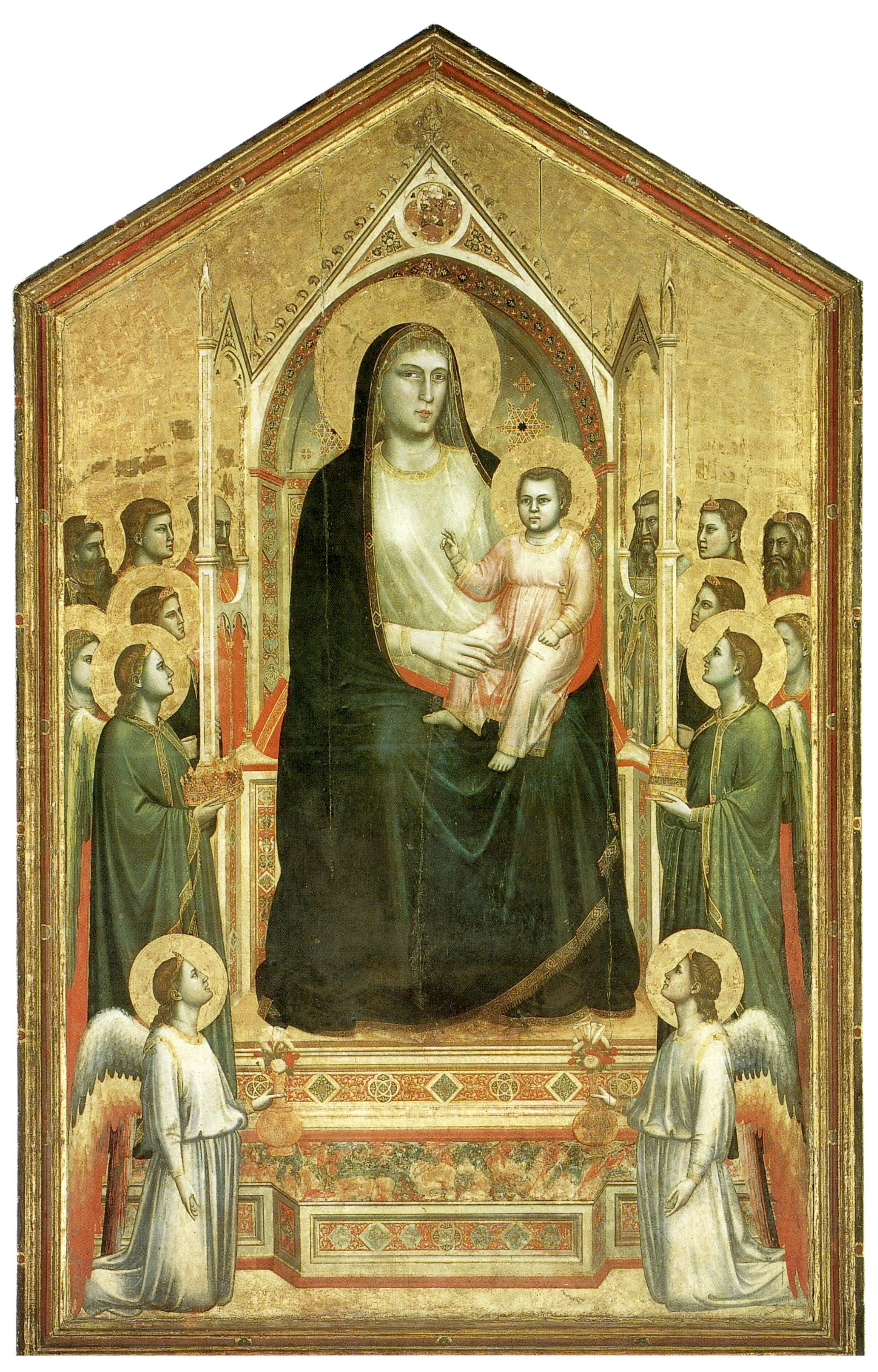

Fra Filippo Lippi

Madonna and Child

(Tarquinia Madonna)

1437

Oil on panel, 45" × 25½" (114.3 × 64.7cm). Galleria Nazionale d'Arte Antica, Rome.

Giorgio Vasari, the sixteenth-century Italian architect/art historian, wrote that Fra Filippo Lippi (c. 1406–1469) decided to become a painter at the age of nineteen after Lippi observed the great Florentine painter Masaccio at work in the Brancacci Chapel. Painted for the ancient Etruscan city of Tarquinia, Lippi's *Madonna and Child*, powerfully modeled by direct light, shows his assimilation of Masaccio's techniques. A striking personal touch of naturalism is the absence of a halo for either of the sacred figures. Lippi's Madonna is a much less aristocratic figure than Giotto's: she is not stiffly enthroned, but leans toward the Child, while the background reveals a domestic scene with a bed. By presenting the Madonna surrounded by realistic details, Lippi emphasizes the similarity between Mary and the many other mothers on earth.

Celebrations in Art

Mothers & Children

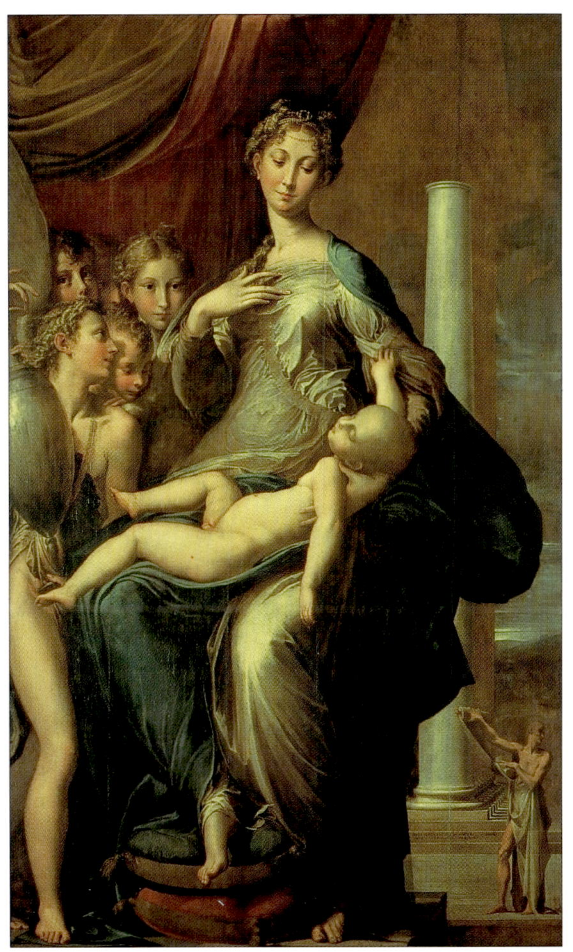

Roxana Marcoci

MetroBooks

MetroBooks
AN IMPRINT OF FRIEDMAN/FAIRFAX PUBLISHERS

ISBN 1-56799-162-9

Editor: Sharyn Rosart
Production Editor: Loretta Mowat
Art Director: Jeff Batzli
Designers: Lynne Yeamans & Lori Thorn
Photography Editor: Wendy Missan

Colour separations by Bright Arts (Singapore) Pte. Ltd.
Printed in China by Leefung-Asco Printers Ltd.

Additional Photography Credits: page 1: Pablo Picasso, *Mother and Child*, 1921. Oil on canvas, 56½" × 64" (143.5 × 162.5cm). The Art Institute of Chicago. Page 2: Mary Cassatt, *The Bath*, 1891–1892. Oil on canvas, 39½" × 26" (100.3 × 66cm). The Art Institute of Chicago. Page 3: Parmigianino, *Madonna of the Long Neck*, 1534–1540. Oil on wood, 85" × 52" (215.9 × 132cm). Galleria degli Uffizi, Florence, Erich Lessing/ Art Resource, NY. Page 5: Marguerite Gérard, *Sleep my Child*, c. 1783–1785. Oil on canvas, 21⅝" × 17¾" (55 × 45cm). Staatliche Kunsthalle Karlsruhe, Germany.

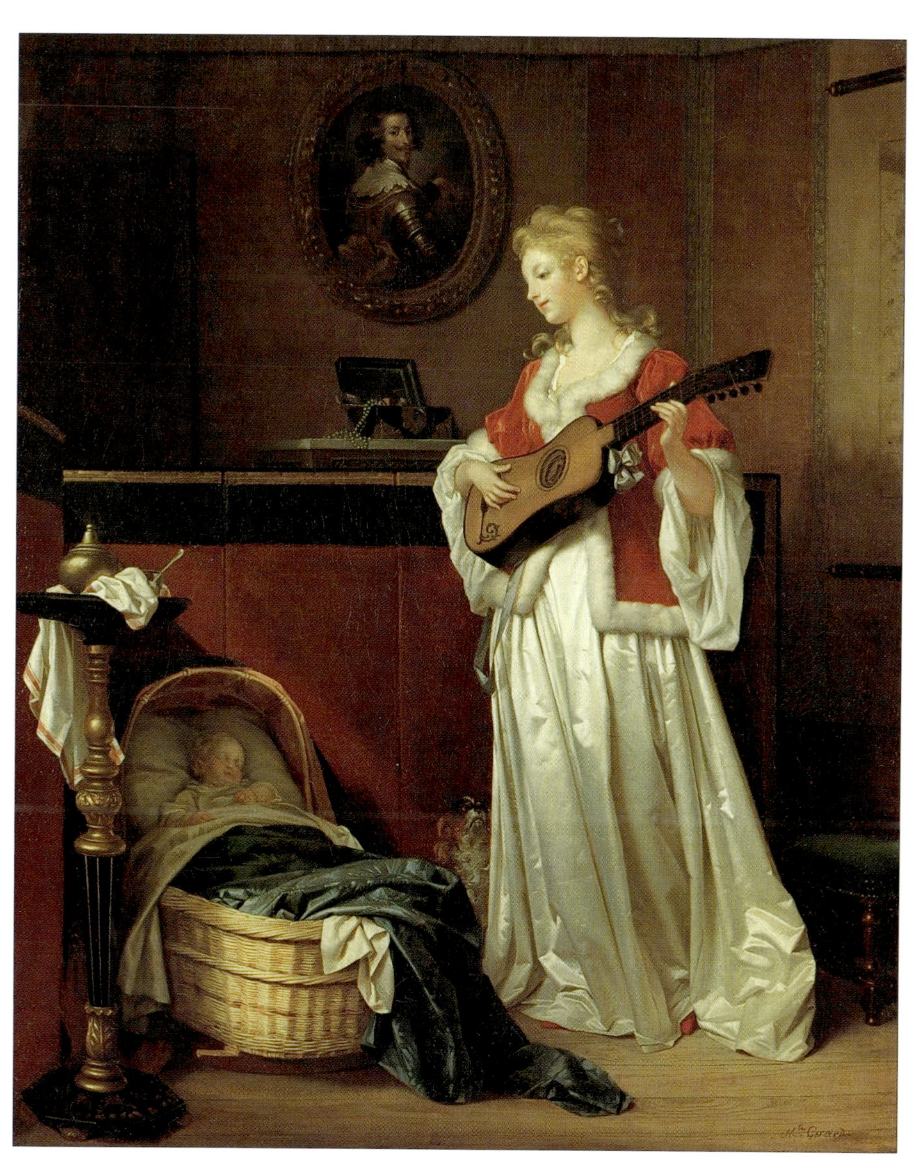

Introduction

The image of mother and child, with its nuances of warmth, nurturing, and unconditional love, evokes a powerful emotional response in all of us. It is not surprising that such a universally compelling image should be central to the development of Western art—from medieval altarpieces that feature the Madonna and Child to secular representations of the female body during the modern age.

Numerous cultures have chosen to represent femininity with maternal motifs, and Christianity in particular sponsored many such images. Trecento (fourteenth-century) artists like Giotto di Bondone and Duccio di Siena compressed the fullness and perfection of motherhood into the image of the Virgin Mary. From her earliest depictions onward, the Virgin has been represented as a protective figure cradling the Infant in her arms, often nursing him, and through him implicitly caring for the well-being of all Christians. Thus, the image of the nursing mother came to be invested with the symbolism of life, particularly during the Middle Ages and the Renaissance when infant survival depended on access to breast milk and proper nourishment. The image of the nursing Virgin also conveys a message about Mary's humanity, accessibility, and emotional richness.

The earliest Western representation of the Virgin nursing the Christ Child appears on the facade of Santa Maria Trastevere in Rome, a twelfth-century mosaic in which the regal posture of Mary clearly conveys her function as Queen of Heaven. As we advance into the thirteenth century, the Virgin's regal image as *Maria Regina* is supplemented by the maternal aspect of the Holy Mother. Soon afterward, the first representations of Mary as a simple, modest, and devoted mother marked a shift from a transcendental to a more humanist sensibility. The humanization of Christianity through the cult of the mother inspired one of the greatest Tuscan painters of the Renaissance, Piero della Francesca, to depict Mary in his celebrated *Nativity* (1470) kneeling in front of her newborn child, thus underscoring the Virgin's closeness to women's real-life experiences. About this time, the Virgin acquired the more earthly, feudal title of *Notre Dame*, or Our Lady, and her popularity with the masses resulted in the proliferation of churches dedicated to Mary.

Beginning with the early decades of the fourteenth century, artists began treating the motif of the Madonna and Child with a new sense of domestic intimacy. The Virgin was portrayed in more naturalistic terms, and the actual site of her home was no longer the heavenly throne, but rather the cozy middle-class interior. The intimacy and tenderness of these domestic scenes, whether by Andrea di Bartolo, the Master of Flémalle, or Sandro Botticelli, contributed to the Virgin's influence as a model for actual women. Depictions of the nursing Virgin signified not only the (super)natural power to conceive, but also the social power to nourish, shelter, and sustain human life. In fact, during this period, the Virgin was one of the few female figures to have attained the status of myth—she came to embody the image of the archetypal mother.

As the Renaissance ended, nonreligious depictions of the mother-and-child motif became popular as well, particularly those by sixteenth- and seventeenth-century Dutch and Flemish painters and French engravers. These artists reinterpreted the motif within the middle-class household and its family life. Before the sixteenth century, interior scenes were extremely rare. But the interest later taken in genre scenes prompted the revival of motherhood within the specific context of the happy family. The image of the contented mother reflected a change from the concept of family as a genealogical line, or chain of descendants, to the birth of the modern family as the basic organizational unit of society. The charm of the simple, domestic life, coupled with the warmth and intimacy of a mother's relationship with her children, became the subject of numerous scenes by such Dutch artists as Gerard Dou, Pieter de Hooch, and Gerard Ter Borch. These scenes portrayed ordinary people rather than religious figures. They celebrated the middle-class household and its members, particularly the mother, who was perceived as a down-to-earth, respectable teacher of her children.

The new structure of the modern family was also instrumental in challenging old notions of child rearing. During the eighteenth century, French artists influenced by the Enlightened thinkers and the Encyclopedists began conveying images of child care and education that radically subverted popular practices. As the century wore on, the more progressive strata of the bourgeoisie and eventually members of the aristocracy adopted the task of nursing and personally caring for their offspring with a new sense of love and responsibility. In his numerous genre scenes, French painter Jean-Baptiste Siméon Chardin explored issues of child rearing with both warmth and seriousness. One of his most effective pictures, *Saying Grace* (1740), deals with the religious framework of family life. According to custom, in the absence of a priest, it was the youngest boy in the household who was supposed to bless the table at the beginning of the meal. In his treatment of the theme, Chardin combined three ideas: the mother's role in the dissemination of private religious worship, the central function played by the child, and the significance of the family's gathering around the meal. Thus, the theme of grace became not only a model for family praying, but moreover one that had been directly appropriated from the iconography of the Holy Family.

Another motif that became very popular during the second half of the eighteenth century was that of the happy or good mother, a theme fully developed by Jean Baptiste Greuze in his painting *The Beloved Mother* (1765). Greuze depicted the virtuous mother as representing the most natural state of womanhood. Influenced by the thinkers of the Enlightenment and particularly by the philosophical doctrines of Jean-Jacques Rousseau, Greuze was instrumental in promoting a set of moral precepts according to which a woman's sole source of true fulfillment was believed to lie in motherhood. In fact, French philosophers, artists, and educators from the eighteenth century in general agreed that it was the domestic life that offered the most natural and happy career for the woman, who was defined as the vital link between father and child.

Even more than Greuze, Jean-Honoré Fragonard portrayed in his art the ideal of the happy family. Like his contemporaries, Fragonard was the heir to the Dutch and Flemish legacy. His paintings of women and children executed in collaboration with his student and sister-in-law, Marguerite Gérard, were informed by such works as Peter Paul Rubens' *Helena Fourment and Her Children* (c. 1636). With Rococo fervor, Fragonard and Gérard depicted a whole series of fashionable women enjoying every aspect of motherhood, from the experience of breast-feeding to the rewards of receiving a child's kisses. Like most of their contemporaries, these artists believed that the new family, at once more intimate and structured than the old, better served the educational and psychological needs of children. The home, the family, and particularly its unifying element, the wife-mother, came to be regarded as the locus of warmth and tranquility in contrast to the cold and harsh reality of the outside world.

Thus, the cult of motherhood, which had conquered the imagination of the bourgeoisie, soon spread to other social strata, especially the aristocracy. Commissioned portraits by women of noble rank reflected their interest in being represented as affectionate mothers. British artists like Sir Joshua Reynolds, Thomas Gainsborough, and George Romney are well known for their portrayals of the aristocracy and for conveying the relationship between mothers and children with freshness and lyric grace. In contrast to most society portraitists of the eighteenth century, these artists went past the mere depiction of formal decorum to evoke the intimacy, charm, and beauty of the mother-child bond. In *Lady Cockburn and Her Three Eldest Sons* (1773), Sir Joshua Reynolds celebrated the image of motherhood by translating an everyday scene into the realm of pagan mythology. Reynolds used the figure of Charity as a model for Lady Cockburn, and that of Cupid for her children, in order to create a harmonious group and a pyramidal structure through which he could comment on the need for stability and order within society.

At the age of twenty-seven, Marie-Louise-Elisabeth Vigée-Lebrun began painting the first of her many portraits of Queen Marie-Antoinette of France. In 1787, Vigée-Lebrun presented at the Salon an affectionate portrait of the queen posed with her children. The work, which became the royal icon of motherhood, is articulated across an ideological shift. Instead of the historical portrait typical of the ancient regime, the artist constructed the ideal image of a mother's rapport with her children. Drawing from the Madonna and Child tradition, Vigée-Lebrun in effect re-created the Holy Family on royal ground. Her interest in the official and somewhat propagandistic representation of the queen as an affectionate mother aside, Vigée-Lebrun should be remembered as one of the few women artists who seriously addressed the issue of a woman's dual identity prior to the twentieth century. In her self-portraits with her daughter, Vigée-Lebrun made a point of revealing herself as both devoted mother and professional artist, roles that in eighteenth-century society were defined as mutually exclusive.

In Victorian England, given the matriarchal influence of the queen and her belief in the important role played by children in society, there was a campaign for moral reforms. The Pre-Raphaelite Brotherhood of 1848 presented the mother-and-child image as an antidote to the ethical diseases of the contemporary society. Works by Sir John Everett Millais, Ford Madox Brown, and Dante Gabriel Rosetti charted the emergence of a moralistic and emotionally loaded image of the family in which domesticity was paramount.

During the nineteenth century, expressions of the mother-and-child-centered culture became enormously popular throughout French society. Among the many Impressionist variations on the theme are the noteworthy paintings of Mary Cassatt and Berthe Morisot. These artists' own experiences with the domestic space are presented in works that delineate the social, sexual, and psychological construction of femininity across the various stages of women's lives. While sharing the popular cult of motherhood with their male colleagues Manet, Degas, Monet, Renoir, and Bazille, these two female painters differed in their refusal to objectify the feminine sphere. Works such as Cassatt's *The Bath* (1891–1892) and Morisot's *Mother and Sister of the Artist* (1870) define the roles of women, from the cradle through young motherhood to maturity, in a traditional way. Yet while still bound to the historical definition of femininity as exclusively domestic and maternal, both Cassatt and Morisot present remarkably perceptive depictions of the female experience in its difference and its specificity.

Images of mother and child continue to resonate in today's society, in which the role of women is hotly debated. One's views aside, the emotional power and beauty of these images is indisputable.

GIOTTO DI BONDONE

Madonna and Child Enthroned

c. 1310

OIL ON PANEL, 128" × 80¼" (325.1 × 203.8CM). GALLERIA DEGLI UFFIZI, FLORENCE.

The Virgin Mary with Child was a popular subject in the Middle Ages, when painters were often commissioned to create works for churches. *Madonna and Child Enthroned* was painted by the great Florentine artist Giotto (c. 1266–1337) for the high altar of the Church of Ognissanti. The architectural severity of the Gothic throne encloses the Virgin and Child on three sides, thus insulating them from the rest of the world. The two foremost angels offer Mary a golden box and a crown, calling attention to the identity of the Virgin as Queen of Heaven. The two kneeling angels before the throne present to the Virgin lilies and roses, which represent her chastity and charity. In order to remove the scene from ordinary experience, Giotto made use of a golden background. The image of Christ's mother as a queen dates as far back as the sixth century.

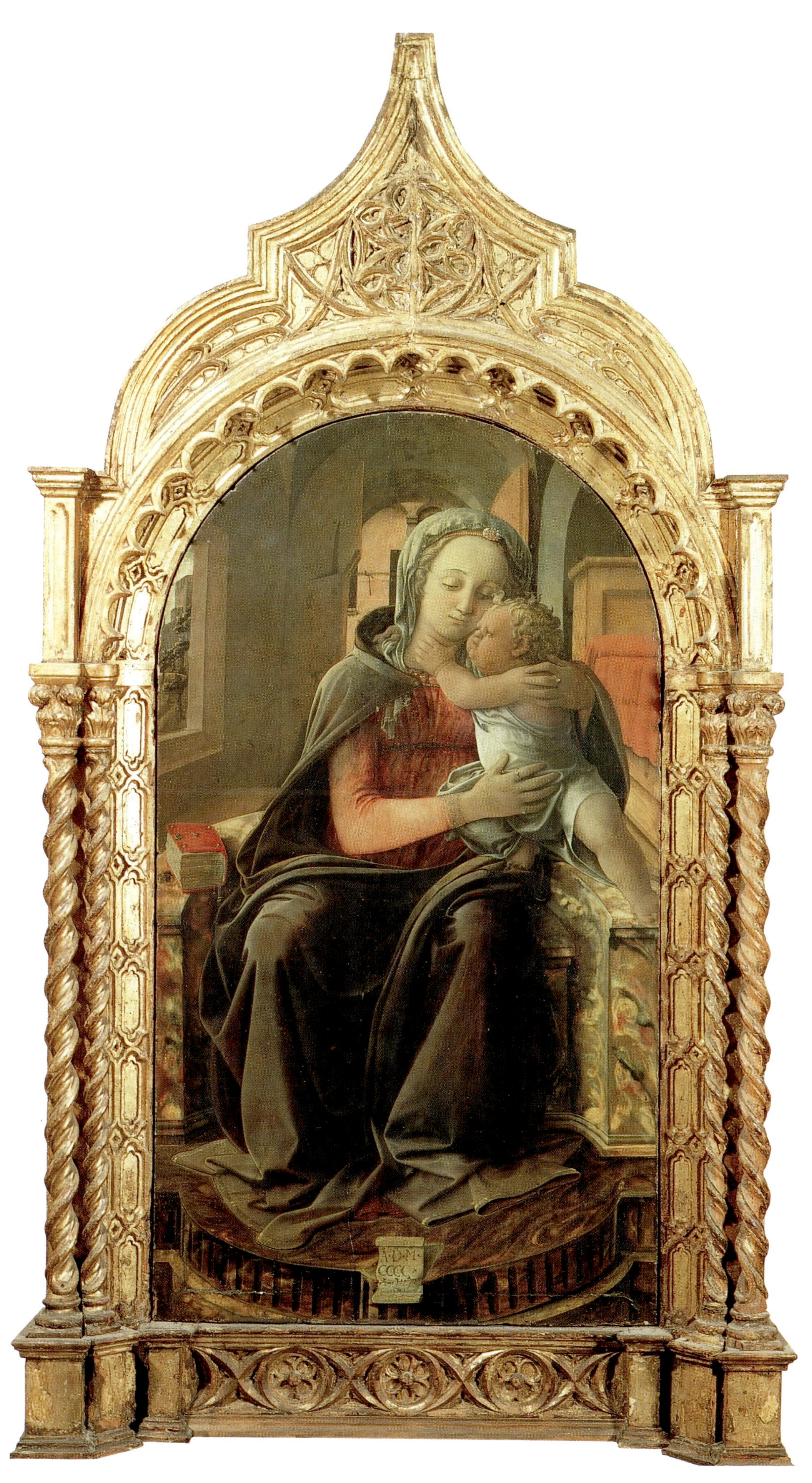

Hans Memling

Madonna and Child with Angels

c. 1479

Oil on panel, $22^{5/8}$" × $18^{1/4}$" (57.6 × 46.4cm). National Gallery of Art, Washington, D.C.

The most admired Flemish artist in the last quarter of the fifteenth century was Hans Memling (c. 1430–1494). Although indebted to the legacy of Flemish masters Rogier van der Weyden and Hugo van der Goes, Memling was closer in his feeling for clarity of design, rational balance, and order to the Italian Renaissance painters Fra Angelico and Raphael. In the 1480s, Memling began developing a form of Northern monumentality that is thoroughly expressed in *Madonna and Child with Angels*. The two musician-angels frame the throne on which the Virgin is sitting with the Infant. The throne is placed below an arch decorated with grapes, symbols of the Eucharist. In the background, the view of a peaceful parklike landscape encapsulates this sacred family scene.

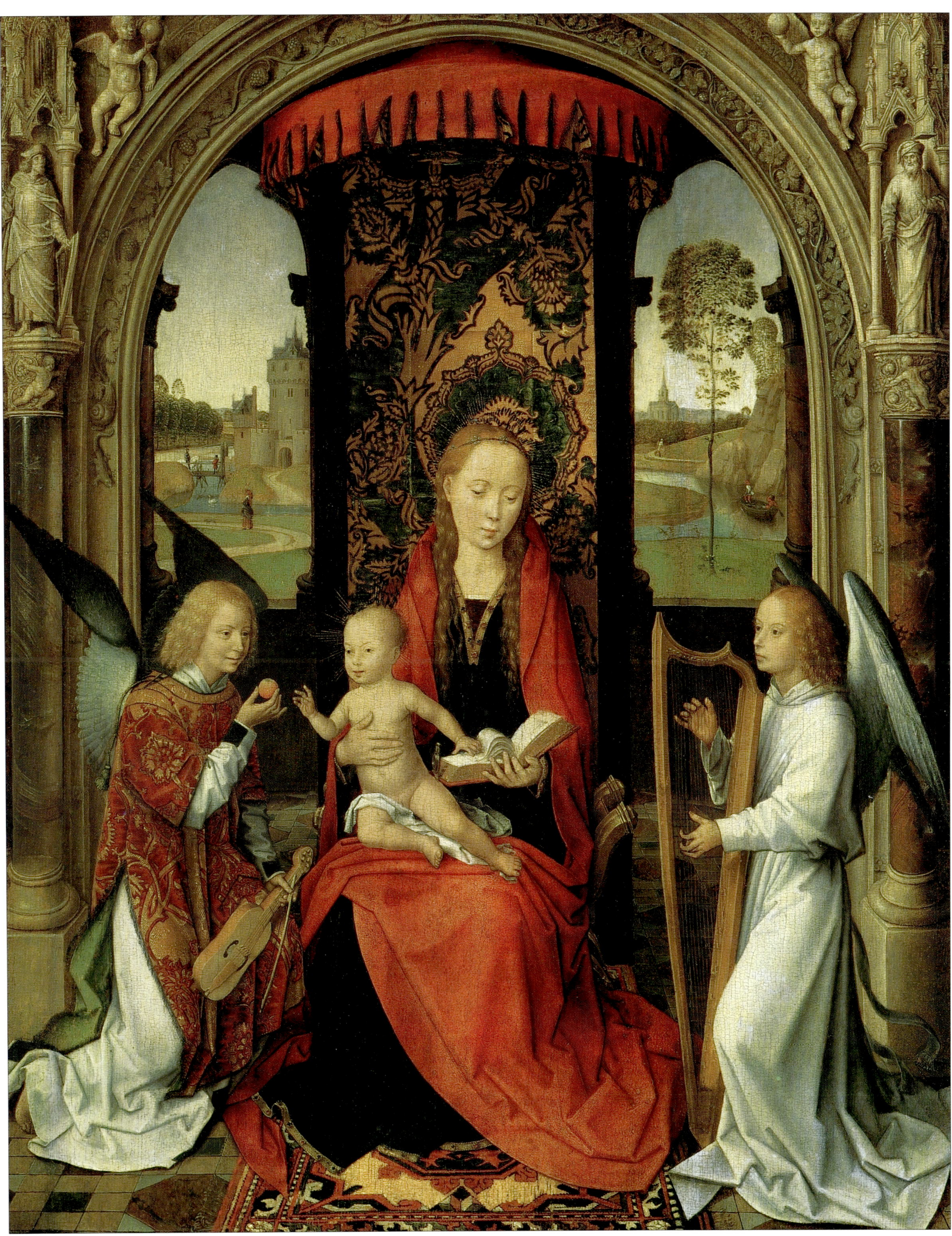

Leonardo da Vinci

Madonna and St. Anne

c. 1501–1513

Oil on panel, 66¼" × 51¼" (168.2 × 130.1cm). Musée du Louvre, Paris.

Madonna and St. Anne is one of the most famous religious group portraits that includes the Virgin, who is shown sitting in the lap of her mother, St. Anne, and reaching for the Christ Child who is breaking away to ride a lamb, the symbol of his sacrificial death. Leonardo (1452–1519) has intertwined the figures to form a living pyramid of communication between the generations. Note that there is little difference in age between St. Anne and her daughter, Mary. Sigmund Freud examined the picture through the lens of psychoanalysis, concluding that the painting was partly inspired by Leonardo's difficulty in reconciling his feelings about his natural mother and his stepmother. Regardless, the painting is a masterly evocation of maternal feeling.

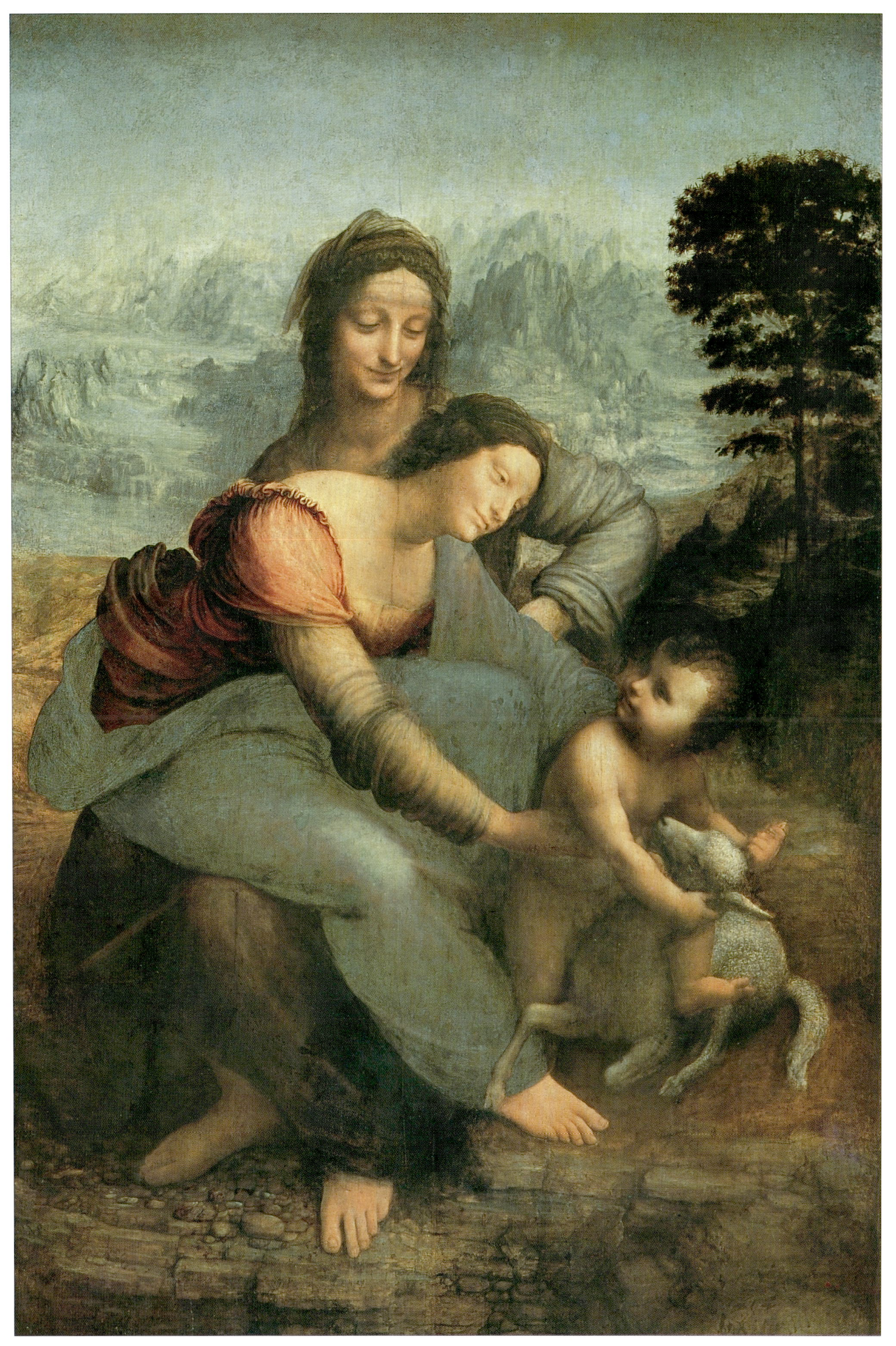

Raphael

Madonna of the Meadows

1505

Oil on panel, 45" × 25½" (114.3 × 64.7cm). Kunsthistorisches Museum, Vienna.

The central painter of the High Renaissance, Raphael (1483–1520) painted numerous Madonnas immediately after he arrived in Florence at the age of twenty-two. The ideals of harmony and beauty characteristic of High Renaissance art are epitomized in Raphael's portraits of the Madonna, which are also known for the serenity of the Madonna's expression. *Madonna of the Meadows*, one of his first explorations of the theme and definitely the finest of the series, contains direct references to the pyramidal family portrait of Leonardo's *Madonna and St. Anne*. The background depicts the Florentine countryside, which is protected by the Virgin, the Christ Child, and the Infant Baptist, patron of the city. The sacred nature of the three figures is suggested by halo shapes reduced to diagrammatic circles of gold, abstract elements that reiterate the allover linearity of this composition.

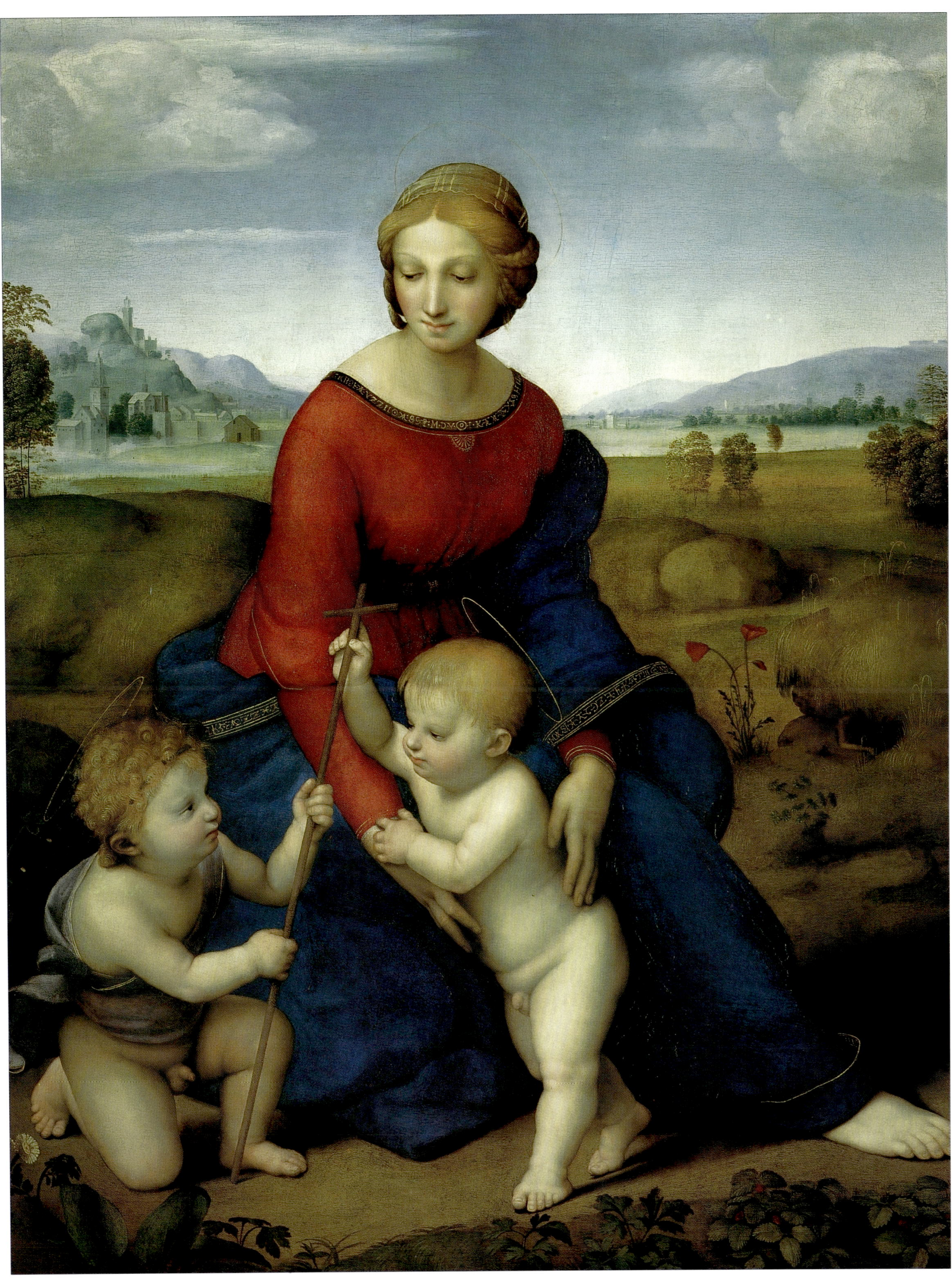

ALBRECHT DÜRER

Madonna with the Slice of Pear

1512

OIL ON PINEWOOD, 19¼" × 14⅝" (60.3 × 37.1CM). KUNSTHISTORISCHES MUSEUM, VIENNA.

Albrecht Dürer (1471–1528), born in Nuremburg, was influenced by the Italian Renaissance during the course of two visits to Italy, including a long stay in Venice. *Madonna with the Slice of Pear* is based on a large study executed by Dürer for another painting, *The Madonna of the Rose Garlands* (1507), which probably represents his most significant work of the Venetian period and established his reputation as a painter. The close proximity between the heads of the Madonna and Child, the pressure of the Child's foot against the breast of his mother, and the turning of his body and head toward her create the dynamics of a composition of exuberant and lively interconnection between the two figures. The soft sfumato (from the Italian for "smoke," referring to a blurring of outlines) of the shadows and the porcelain quality of the Virgin's face anticipate the work of Vermeer, while the vitality of the child figure is truly Michelangelesque in spirit.

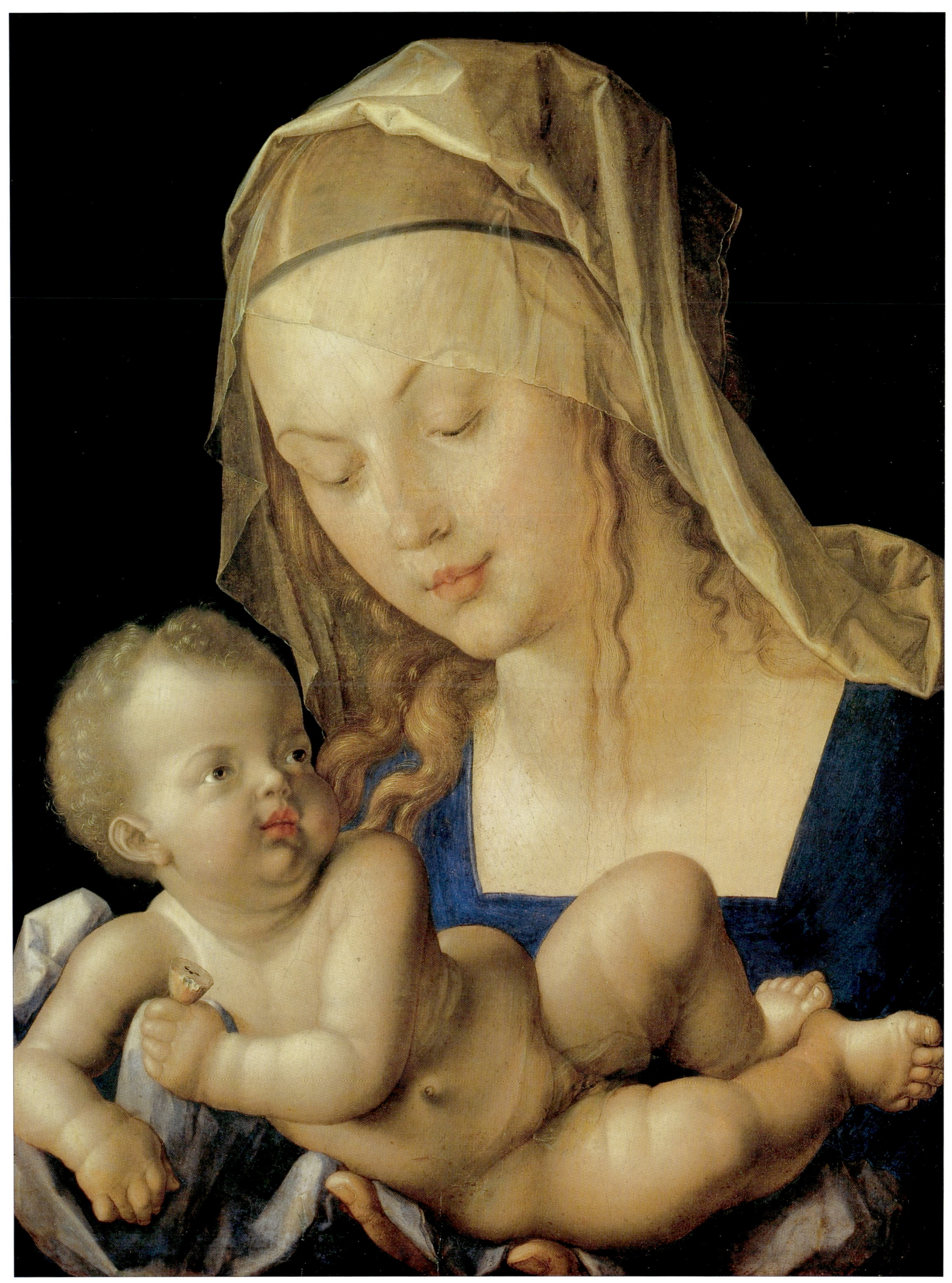

TITIAN

Madonna with a Rabbit

(also called *Madonna and Child with St. Catherine of Alexandria and a Shepherd*)

c. 1529–1530

OIL ON CANVAS, 33" × 27 1/2" (84 × 70 CM). MUSÉE DU LOUVRE, PARIS.

The Venetian Titian (c. 1488–1576), a giant of Renaissance painting, is renowned for both his use of color and his ability to infuse his work with emotion. *Madonna with a Rabbit*, known during the sixteenth century as *Madonna and St. Catherine*, is a picture notable not just for its spiritual quality, but also for its deep sense of humanity. It has been suggested that Titian's wife, Cecilia, may have posed for the figure of the Madonna, while the bearded shepherd in the middle ground may be Federigo Gonzaga, Duke of Mantua, a patron of the arts who had commissioned a number of religious paintings from Titian, including this one. The artist painted the scene with the experience of a man who knew the responsibilities and rewards of a growing family, and who directly witnessed the tenderness of a mother with her child.

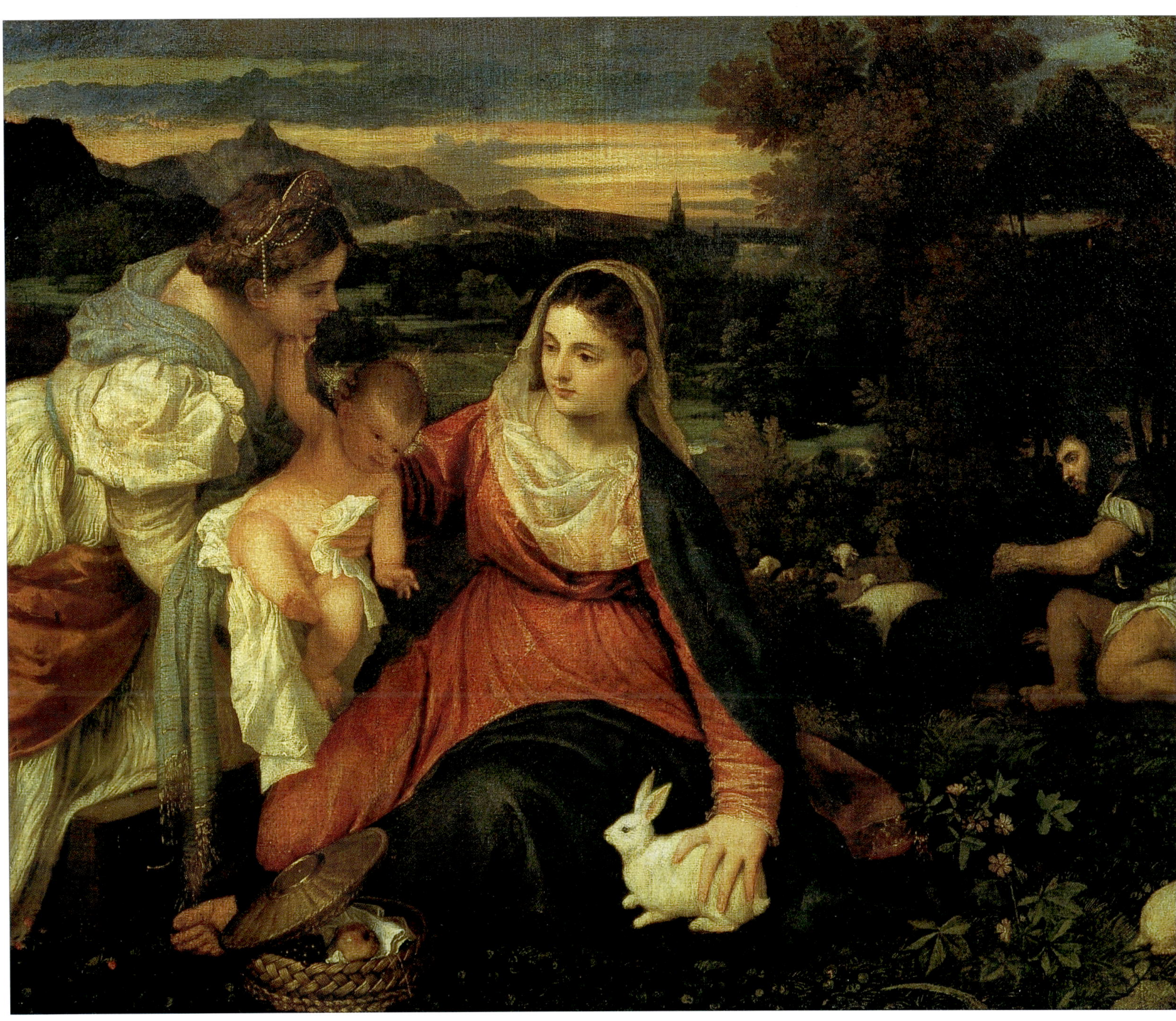

Agnolo Bronzino

Portrait of Eleonora of Toledo with Her Son Giovanni

1550

Oil on panel, 45¼" × 37¾" (114.9 × 95.8cm). Galleria degli Uffizi, Florence.

In 1540, Bronzino (1503–1572) was titled the official painter to the new Medici court under Cosimo I, second duke of Florence and future grand duke of Tuscany. Bronzino developed an elegant International style of Mannerist inflection that greatly appealed to his aristocratic patrons. In this painting of the wife and son of Cosimo I, the artist has produced the model for a type of courtly portrait of gravity and lavishly ornate costume. Mother and child are immediately recognized as members of an exalted social caste, hence their dignified immobility and minimal facial expressions. Yet, for all of Bronzino's chill, he should not be considered an emotionally dry artist. Within the rigid format of the composition, the closeness of the two figures suggests the deep feeling, affection, and nurturing that exist between a mother and her child.

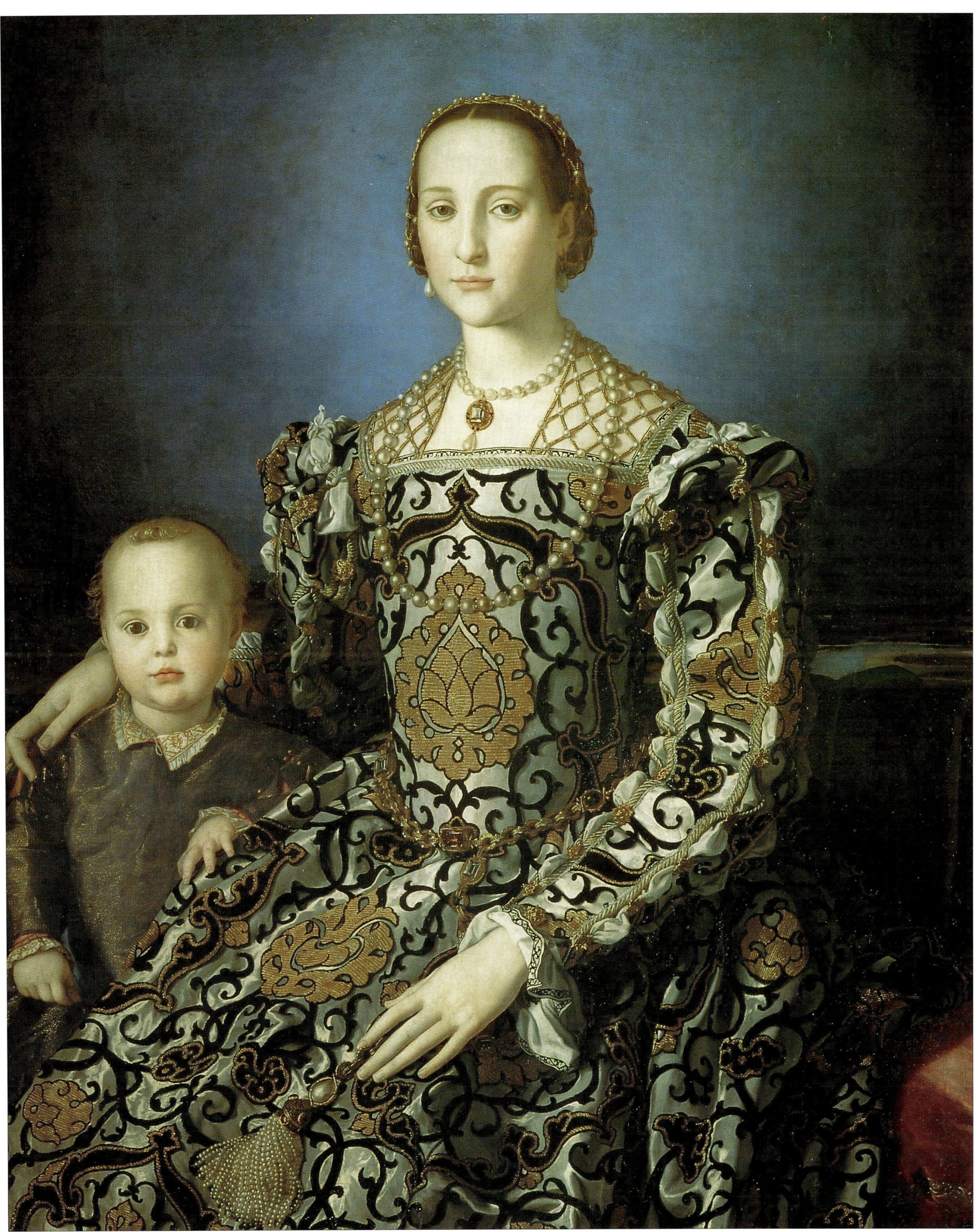

Pieter de Hooch

Woman Nursing an Infant with a Child Feeding a Dog

1658–1660

Oil on canvas, 26 5/8" × 21 13/16" (67.6 × 55.4cm). The Fine Arts Museums of San Francisco.

Pieter de Hooch (1629–c. 1684) is best remembered for his depictions of middle-class Dutch families enjoying the comfort and harmony of the perfect seventeenth-century bourgeois household, and specifically for his penetrating portrayals of the motherly figure. The grouping together of women and children as the nucleus of the family is a recurrent motif in de Hooch's works. In this picture the dialogue between the mother who nurses her infant and the young daughter who feeds the family dog underscores the instrumental role of teaching and imitation in the sphere of domestic life. The dog and the bird within the cage that is suspended from the wall function as references to marital love, fidelity, and housekeeping virtue.

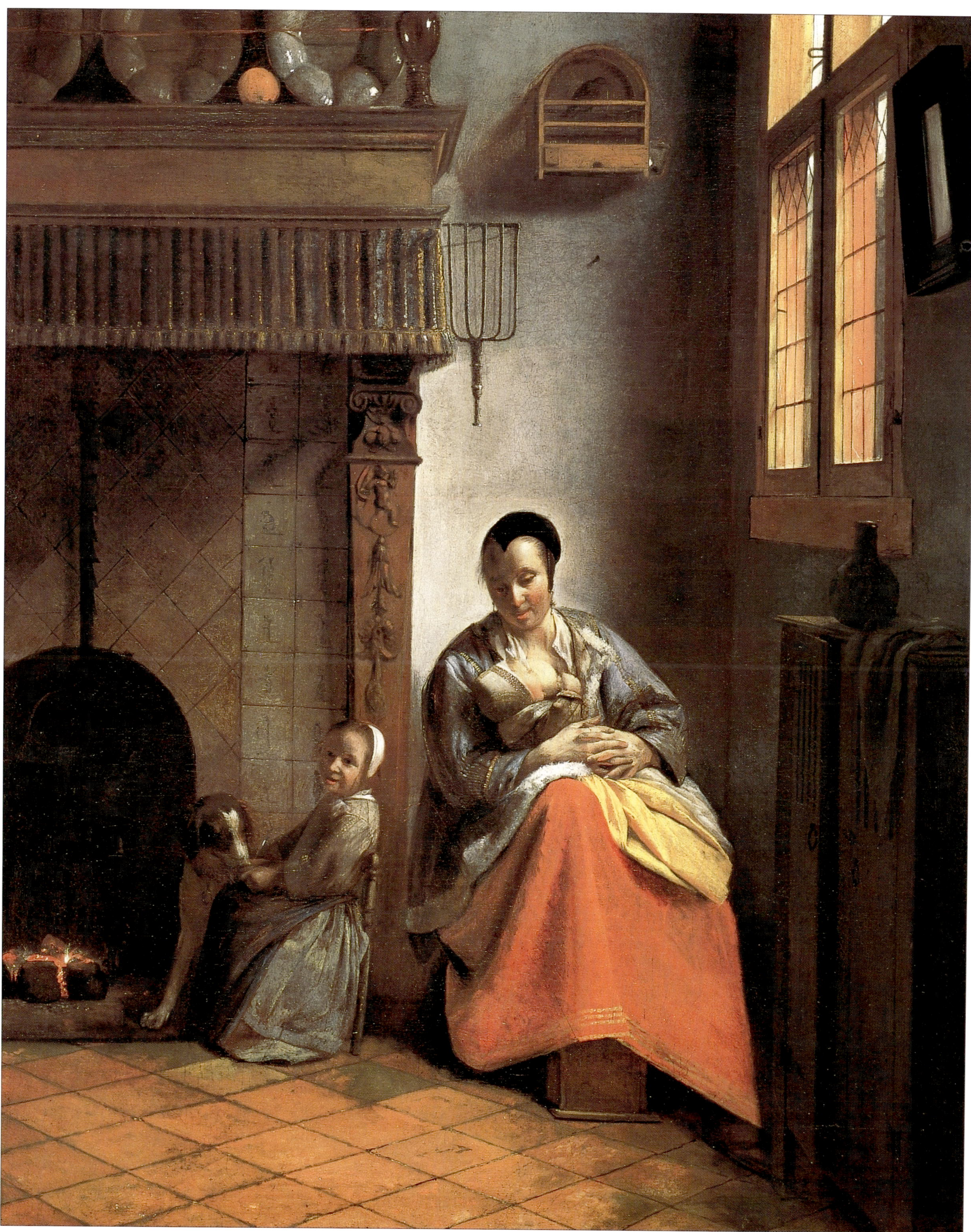

GERARD TER BORCH

Woman Peeling Apples

c. 1660

OIL ON CANVAS, ATTACHED TO PANEL, 14 1/8" × 12" (35.8 × 30.4CM). KUNSTHISTORISCHES MUSEUM, VIENNA.

Along with Johannes Vermeer and Pieter de Hooch, Gerard Ter Borch (1617–1681) is regarded as an innovator in Dutch genre scenes, and is known for his careful, elegant depictions of the lives of the wealthy burghers. This picture is an outstanding example of Ter Borch's fully developed style, which contributed to the conception of a new type of narrative painting of great technical and psychological refinement. *Woman Peeling Apples* is a commentary on parental responsibility. Part of Ter Borch's message is the visual analogy between the ripe fruit that, as the saying goes, rots early, and the harmful effect of forcing a child into premature adulthood, as indicated here by the fancy hat the little girl is wearing. To reinforce this idea, the artist included the candle and map, traditional allusions to the ephemerality of human existence.

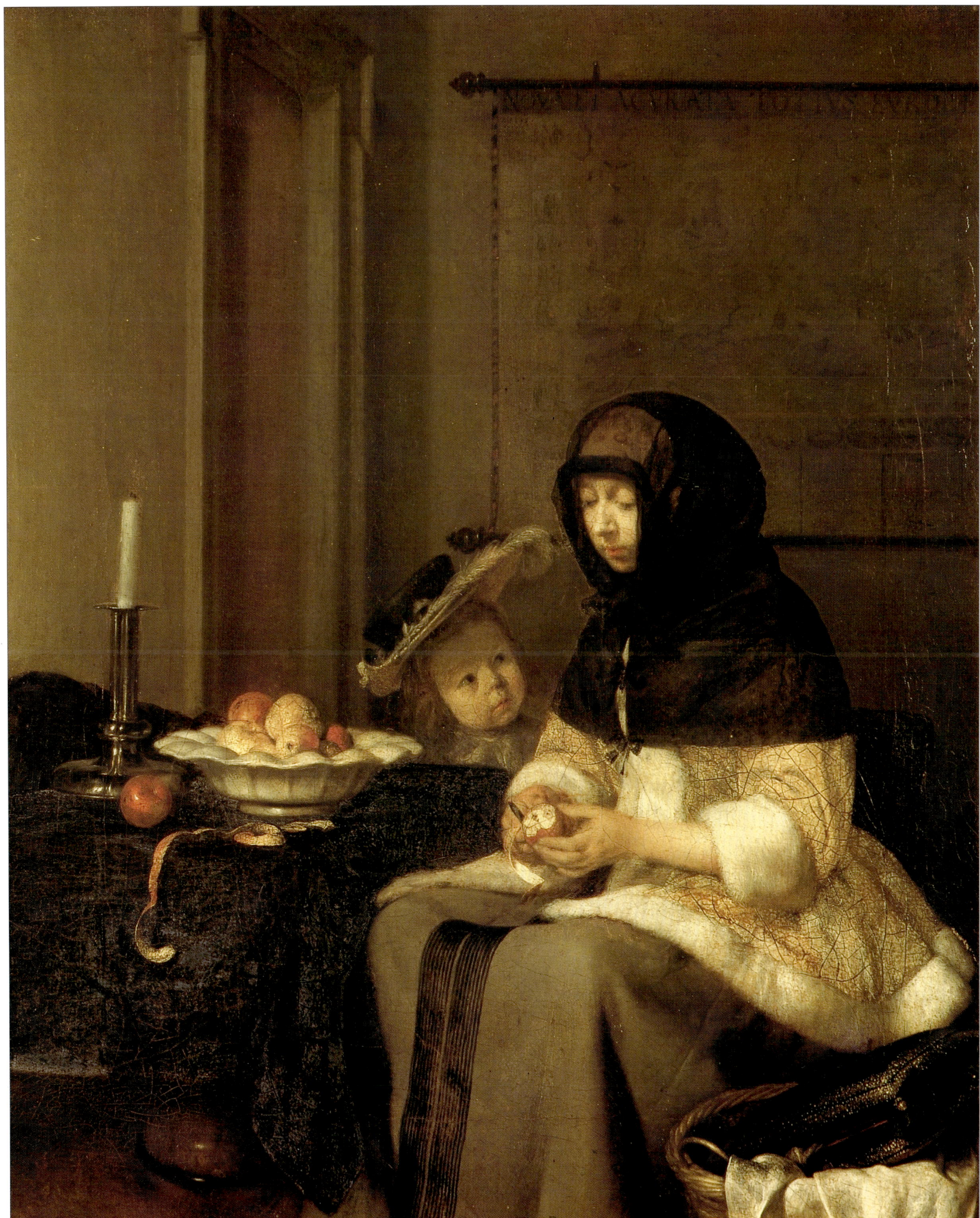

Jean-Baptiste Siméon Chardin

Saying Grace

1740

Oil on canvas, 19½" × 15⅛" (49.5 × 38.5cm). Musée du Louvre, Paris.

In *Saying Grace*, Chardin (1699–1779) invites the viewer into a daily scene filled with great tenderness and human warmth. A young mother feeds her children while teaching them about piety and the sacred nature of the meal. Chardin was the foremost chronicler of the modest and peaceful eighteenth-century middle class and of the honest men and women who found their happiness in the dissemination of family values within their homes. Considered his most popular picture, *Saying Grace* takes its French title, *Le Bénédicte*, from the Latin word for "bless," referring to the blessing of the food that took place right before the meal. Together with *The Diligent Mother* (1740), this work establishes Chardin's affinity and love for the world of children. While avoiding gratuitous sentimentality, the artist has succeeded in translating an ordinary scene into an image of arrested time and truth, finding beauty in the rituals of domestic life.

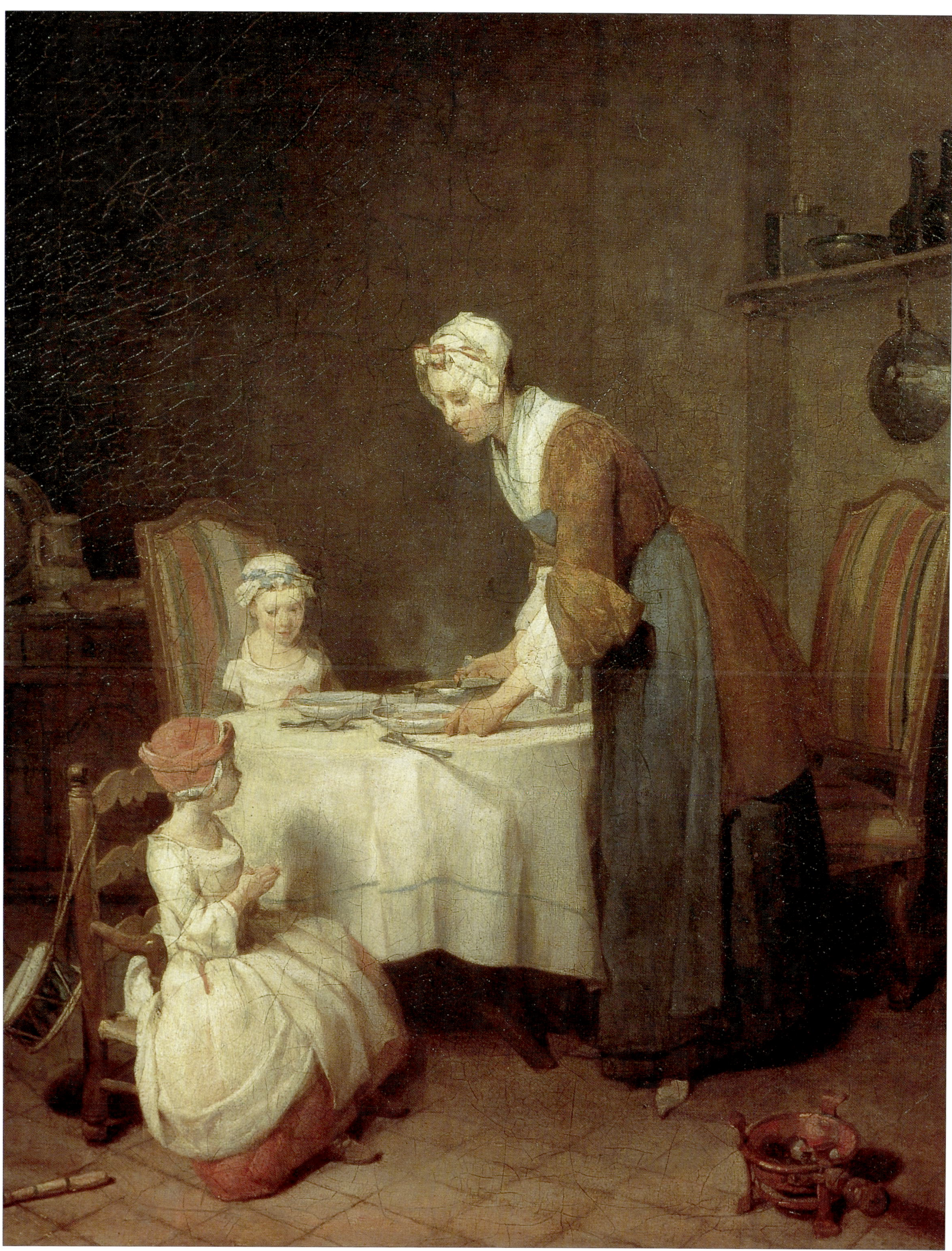

Sir Joshua Reynolds

Lady Cockburn and Her Three Eldest Sons

1773

Oil on canvas, 55¾" × 44½" (141.6 × 113cm). The National Gallery, London.

Unanimously elected the first president of the Royal Academy, Sir Joshua Reynolds (1723–1792) was one of England's greatest portraitists. Among his best female subjects were mothers shown in the aristocratic ambience of the domestic interior. Despite his realistic portrayals, Reynolds often merged contemporary style with that of the ancients. He believed that the classical artists were closer to nature than their modern counterparts, and that classical portraits were imbued with dignity, grace, and an elegiac mood worthy of praise. Reynolds' appreciation for the classics led him to transform English ladies into goddesses, muses, and other mythological figures. For instance, *Lady Cockburn and Her Three Eldest Sons* is derivative in its composition of the Italian allegory of Charity. The children resemble cupids rather than specific individuals, and their mother assumes the stance of a Roman matron. The pyramidal structure of this family group testifies to Reynolds' adherence to the canons of classicism, of which he wrote with great conviction in his treatise on painting, *Discourses*.

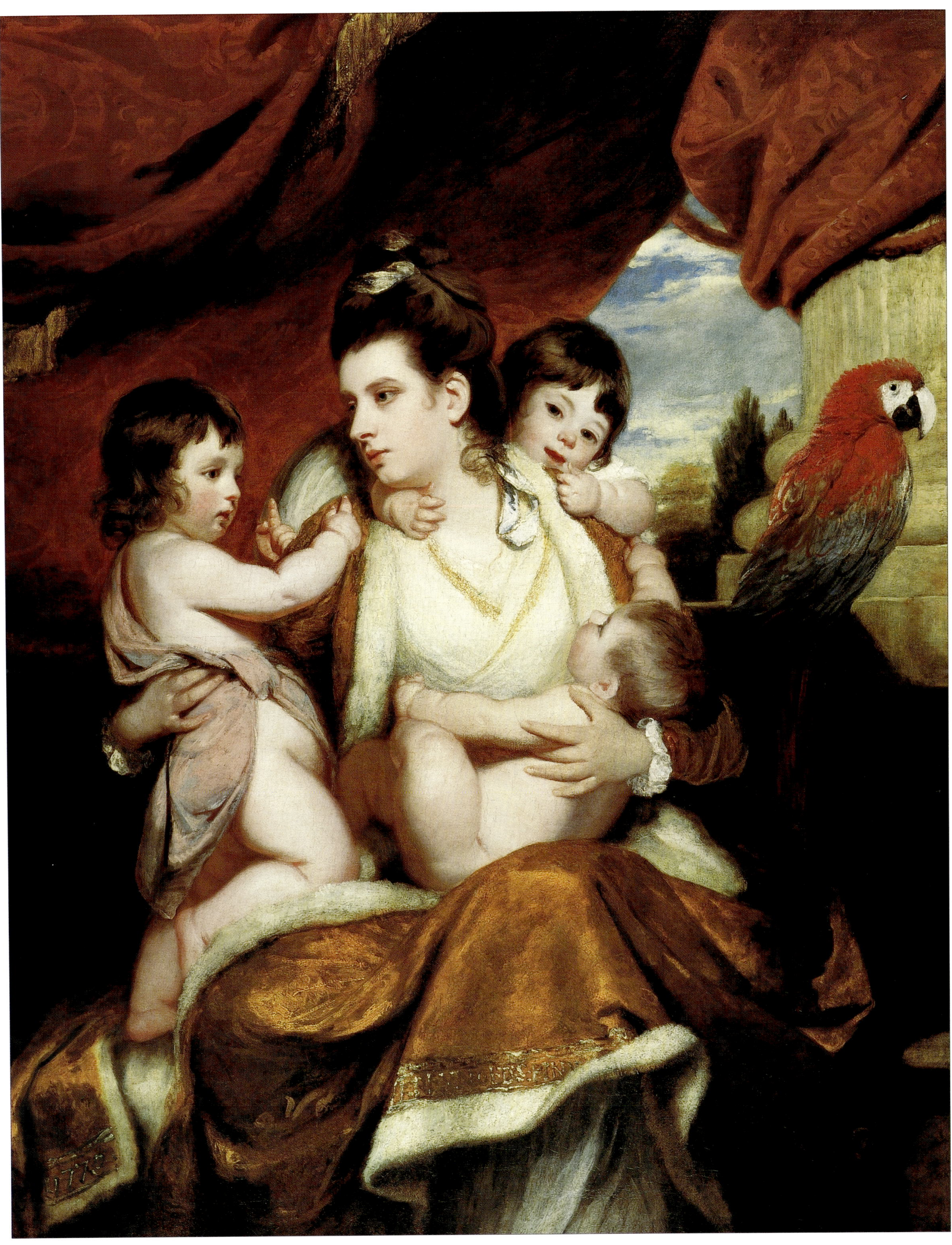

Angelica Kauffmann

Cornelia Pointing to Her Children as Her Treasures

c. 1785

Oil on canvas, 40" × 50" (101.6 × 127cm). Virginia Museum of Fine Arts, Richmond.

The theme of the virtuous mother was a favorite pictorial motif for European artists during the 1780s. In a period shaped by the philosophical writings of moralist Jean-Jacques Rousseau and educator Johann Heinrich Pestalozzi, the issues of child rearing and the role of maternal care were considered at the core of the Neoclassical agenda. Swiss-born Angelica Kauffmann (1741–1807), an erudite woman who was one of the founding members of the Royal Academy in London, found it useful to revive the tale of the second-century Roman mother Cornelia in order to provide her eighteenth-century contemporaries with a moral message. Cornelia refused to remarry after her husband's death, choosing instead to devote herself to the careful upbringing and education of her children. On being shown another woman's precious jewelry, Cornelia pointed at her children and said, "These are my jewels!" Kauffman's painting presents Cornelia, who is holding one of her children by the hand, as an example of the virtues of family life, in contrast to the figure of the seated woman, who is holding a box of jewels in her lap and who represents vice and love of luxury. The artist sought to communicate the importance of motherhood and virtuous behavior via this heroine of classical antiquity.

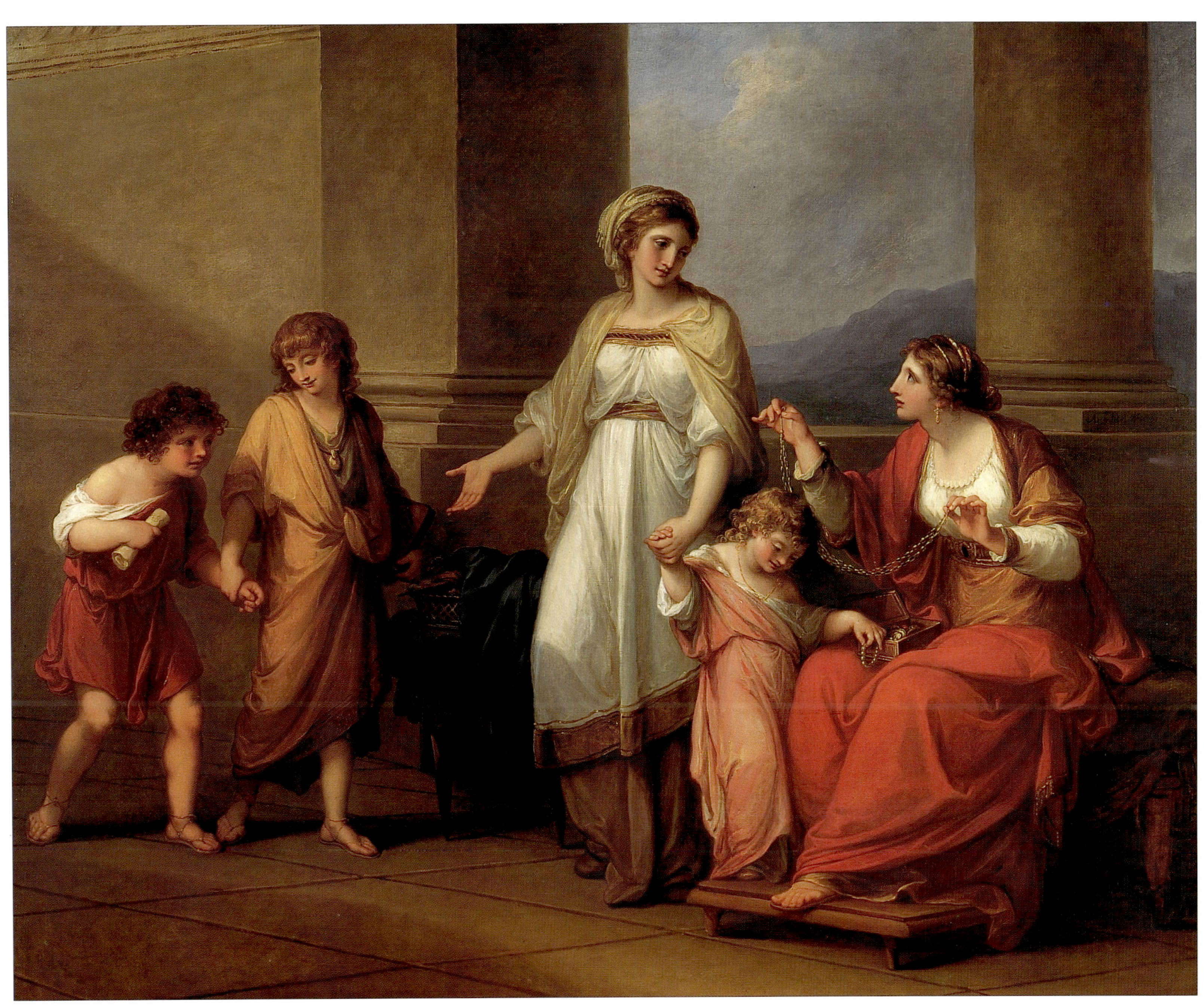

Marie-Louise-Élisabeth Vigée-Lebrun

Marie-Antoinette and Her Children

1787

Oil on canvas, 104" × 82" (264.1 × 208.2cm). Musée National du Château de Versailles et de Trianon.

The image of happy motherhood was such a popular theme in the late eighteenth century that it even touched on the official portraiture of the Queen of France, Marie-Antoinette. Well-known portraitist Marie-Louise-Élisabeth Vigée-Lebrun (1755–1842) was both friend and painter of Marie-Antoinette. This work by Vigée-Lebrun marks a change in the traditional royal portrait insofar as it presents the monarch not as aloof or intimidating, but rather as a gentle mother surrounded by her three children, Marie-Thérèse Charlotte, future Duchesse d'Angoulême; the two-year-old Duc de Normandie, future Louis XVII; and the dauphin. Set in their residence, the Château de Versailles, this group portrait is a variation on the Renaissance theme of the Holy Family. Presented as an icon of royal motherhood, the work's propagandistic message was intended to bridge the gap between the royalty of Versailles and the people of France. After the French Revolution and Marie-Antoinette's death, Vigée-Lebrun traveled widely in Europe, finding subjects for her elegant portraits from England to Russia.

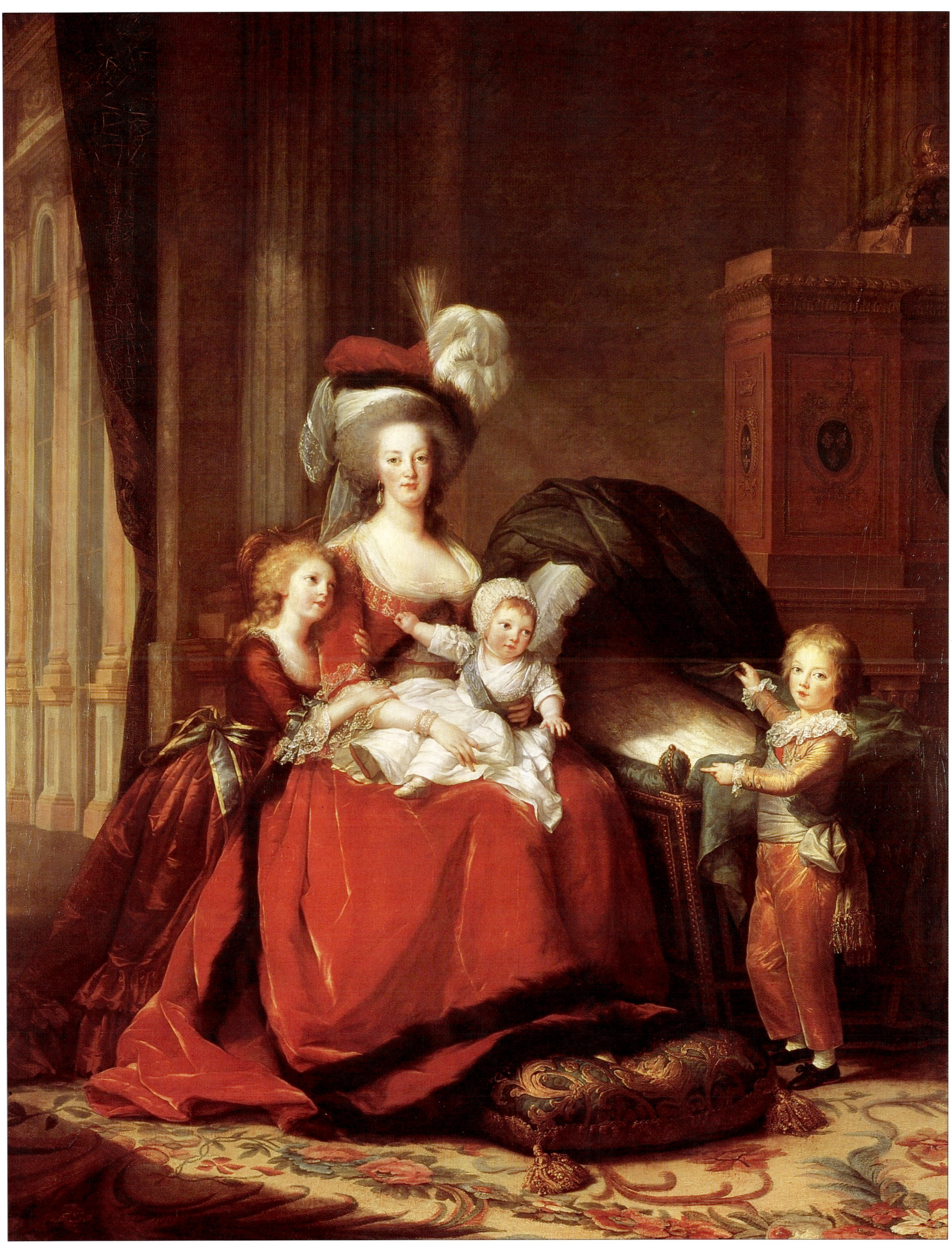

Ford Madox Brown

Pretty Baa-Lambs

1851–1859

Oil on panel, 24" × 30" (60.9 × 76.2cm). Birmingham Museum and Art Gallery, England.

Among the goals of the Pre-Raphaelite Brotherhood, a group of painters and poets who joined together in 1848 to protest the growing materialism of English society, was the intent to depict nature faithfully. Ford Madox Brown (1821–1893) never actually joined the Pre-Raphaelites, but he did share many of their concerns. *Pretty Baa-Lambs* is one of Brown's first outdoor landscape pictures with figures that were modeled after the artist's wife and daughter. The picture, which was exhibited at the Royal Academy in 1852, represents a Victorian interpretation of the Madonna and Child motif. The scenery, painted at Stockwell where Brown was living with his family, is considered one of his most ambitious portrayals of nature. Within the sweeping pastoral landscape, the emphasis is placed on the monumental mother-and-child grouping. The low viewpoint and idiosyncratic facial types are characteristic of Brown's eccentric style. The work, although serene in its sunny atmosphere, was executed at a time when the artist was experiencing financial difficulties and was, in fact, barely capable of feeding and clothing his family.

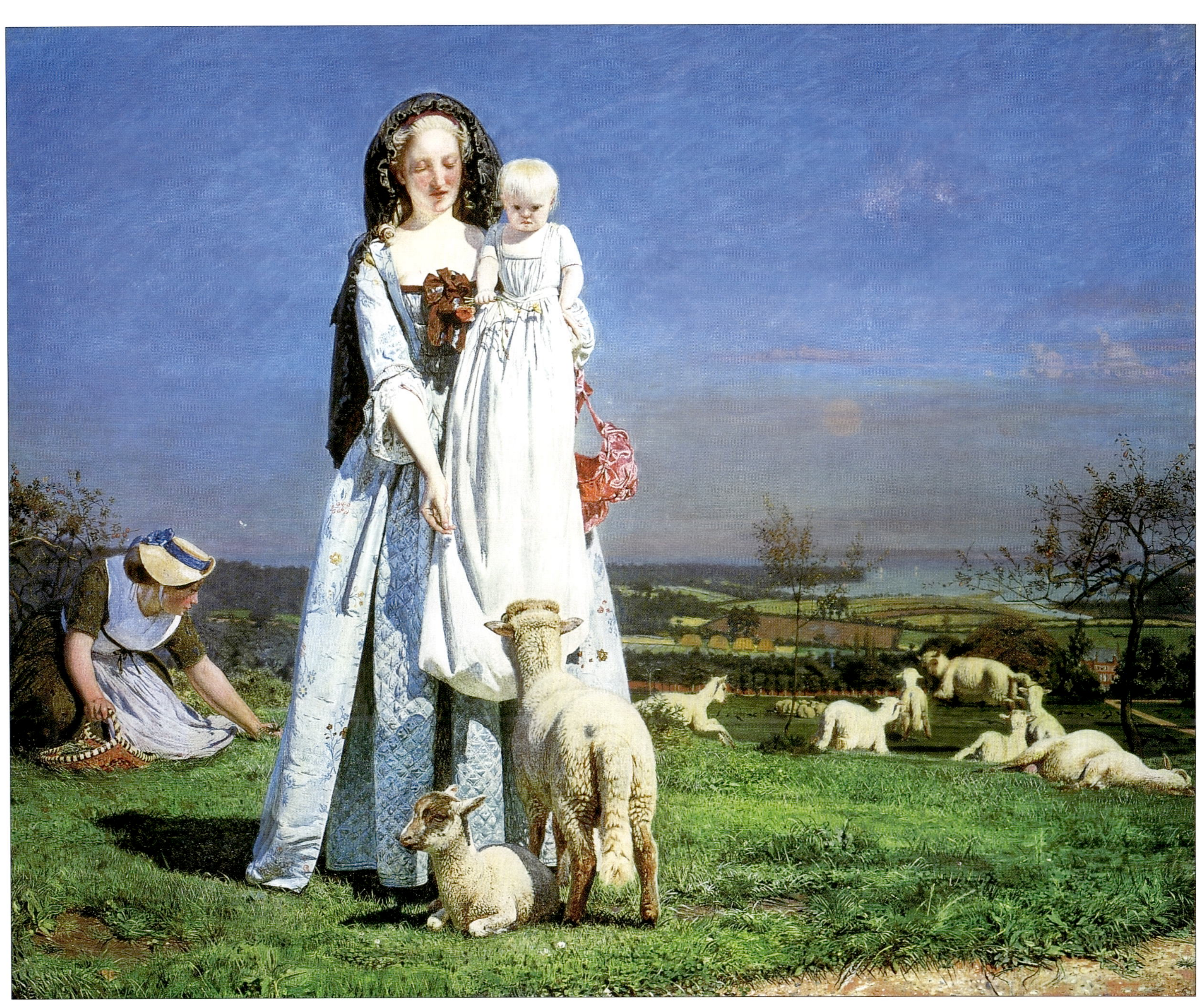

Claude Monet

The Luncheon

1868

Oil on canvas, 90½" × 59" (230 × 150cm). Städelsches Kunstinstitut und Städtische Galerie, Frankfurt.

The Luncheon, one of the very few interiors depicted by Monet (1840–1926), is an inviting and warm picture of the artist's mistress, Camille Doncieux (who became his wife two years later, in 1870), and their one-year-old son, Jean. Although Monet and Doncieux had begun their relationship in 1865, they lived together sporadically, only when they could afford it. This house, situated on the Normandy coast, not far from Monet's native Le Havre, was lent to the couple by a generous patron. In order to emphasize the hospitable nature of his newly found domicile, Monet depicted a sunlit interior with the nicely set luncheon table curving into the viewer's space, as if inviting the viewer to take the vacant chair in the foreground. The focus of the work is the mother with her son, who is shown ready to crack an egg, a sign of his appetite for life.

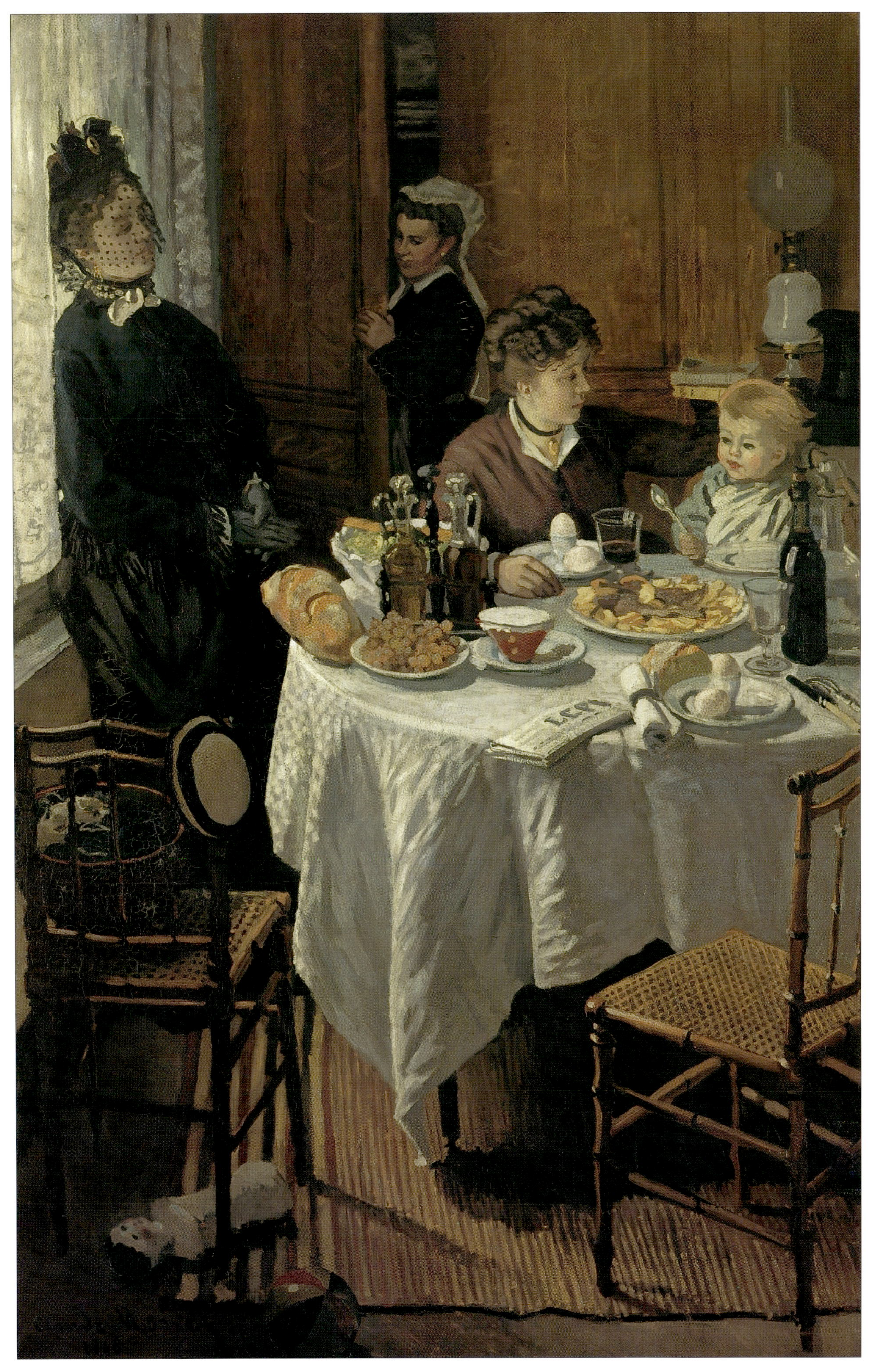

Claude Monet

Wild Poppies

1873

Oil on canvas, 19¾" × 25½" (50.1 × 64.7cm). Musée d'Orsay, Paris.

During the 1870s, Monet often depicted his wife and child in the outdoors, whether in the garden or in the landscape, as extensions of the fields or of flowerbeds. In *Wild Poppies*, the myriad scarlet points of poppies envelop the boy. Like his mother, he is half lost in the plain, becoming almost indistinguishable from his natural surroundings. Camille, Monet's wife, carelessly grasps her parasol, while her son Jean follows her, barely visible in his summer hat. The figures are slowly discovered by the viewer within the matrix of the open land. A close look reveals the same two figures, caught at an earlier moment, atop the hill. Monet's device of developing an interaction between figures and flowers is typical of his other works of the period, with *In the Garden* (1875), *The Artist's Family* (1875), and *In the Meadow* (1876) being the most representative. In each of these pictures there is a vast sense of the fields being gathered into the figures, a sense of diffusion that Monet developed more fully in his late pictures at Giverny.

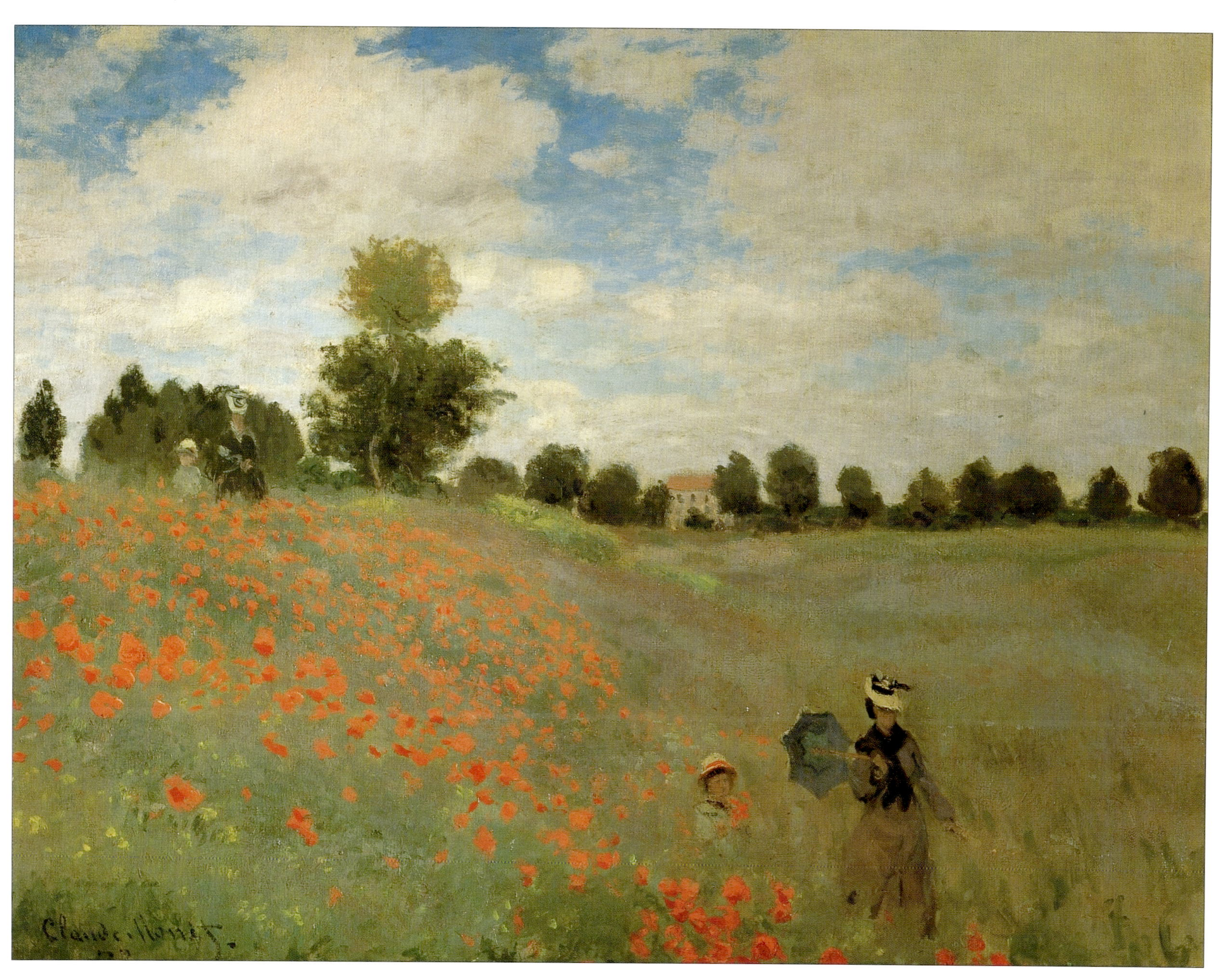
Claude Monet.

Berthe Morisot

Catching Butterflies

1873

Oil on canvas, 18" × 22" (45.7 × 55.8cm). Musée d'Orsay, Paris.

Like Cassatt, Degas, Manet, and Renoir, the French Impressionist Berthe Morisot (1841–1895) explored the essence of modern experience, including aspects of her family life, specifically of the domestic space of femininity. In the early 1870s, Morisot spent summers with her sister's family at Mourecourt. There Morisot executed a series of plein air ("open air") scenes that are the result of her study with the great landscape painter Camille Corot and his pupil Oudinot. Grass, trees, flowers, and foliage are treated with a variety of brush strokes and stenographic notations that indicate Morisot's understanding of the Impressionist stylistic agenda. The work is a portrait of the artist as a motherly figure for her nieces, to whom she was giving a lot of time and attention. The sketchiness of the technique and abstract nature of their facial features, aspects of the work that were denounced by critics at the time, are the same qualities that confirmed Morisot as one of the major female Impressionists. The Irish novelist George Moore praised Morisot's artistic contribution, and stated that without her pictures, a "hiatus" or "blank" would exist in the history of modern art.

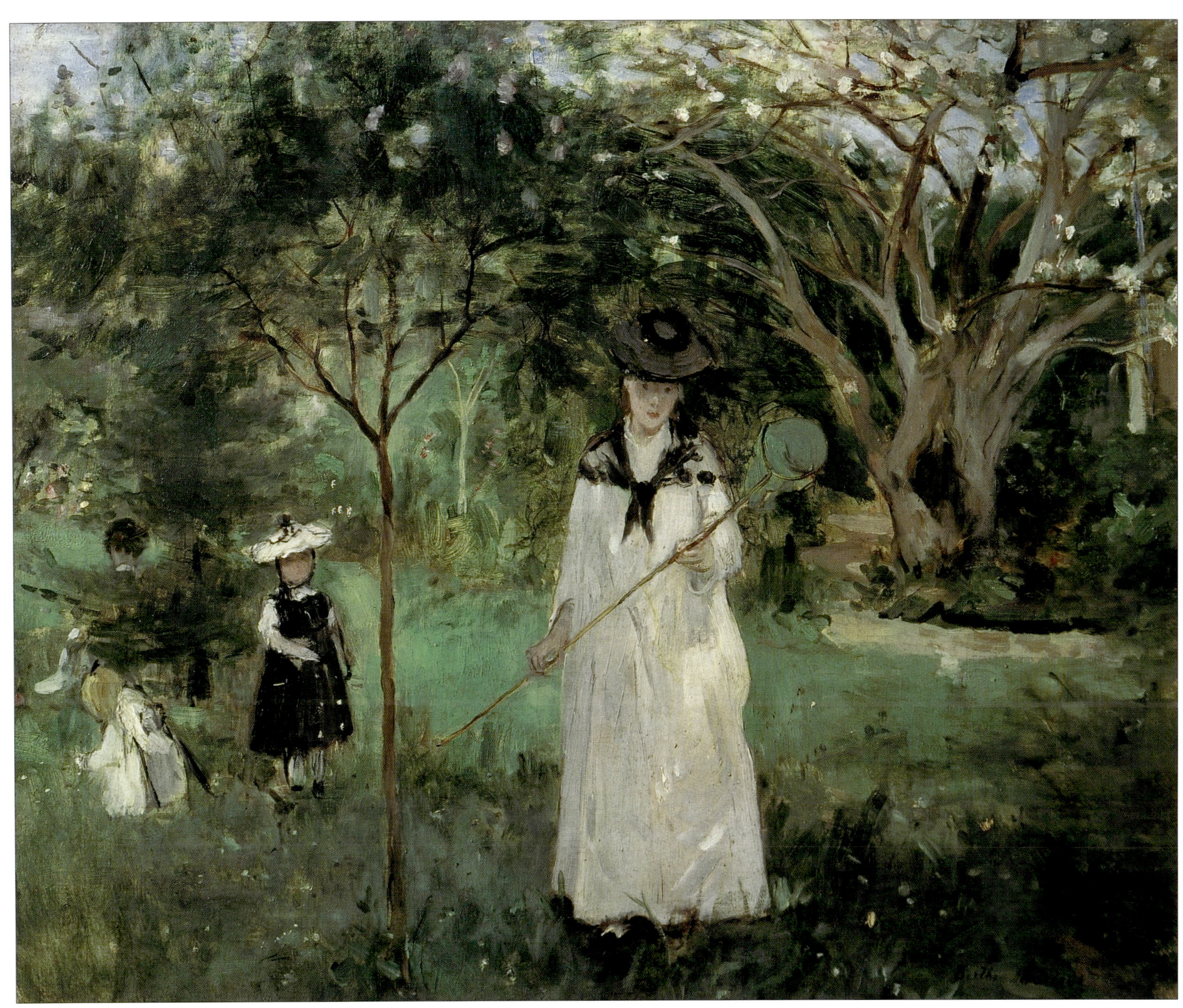

BERTHE MORISOT

The Cradle

1873

OIL ON CANVAS, 22½" × 18½" (57.1 × 47CM). MUSÉE D'ORSAY, PARIS.

The Cradle, one of the most tender and intimate portrayals of maternity, depicts Morisot's sister Edma watching over her sleeping baby daughter. During this period, the mother-and-child motif appealed very strongly to the popular imagination, often being raised to an almost religious significance. This painting was shown at the first Impressionist exhibition in 1874 and demonstrates Morisot's ability to use a freely applied, spontaneous brush stroke to convey a mood of intimacy and directness that underscores her experimental technique. Opposing the classical lessons of her first teacher, Guichard, the artist comes closer in sensibility to the more radical vision of her friend and mentor (and later, brother-in-law), Edouard Manet.

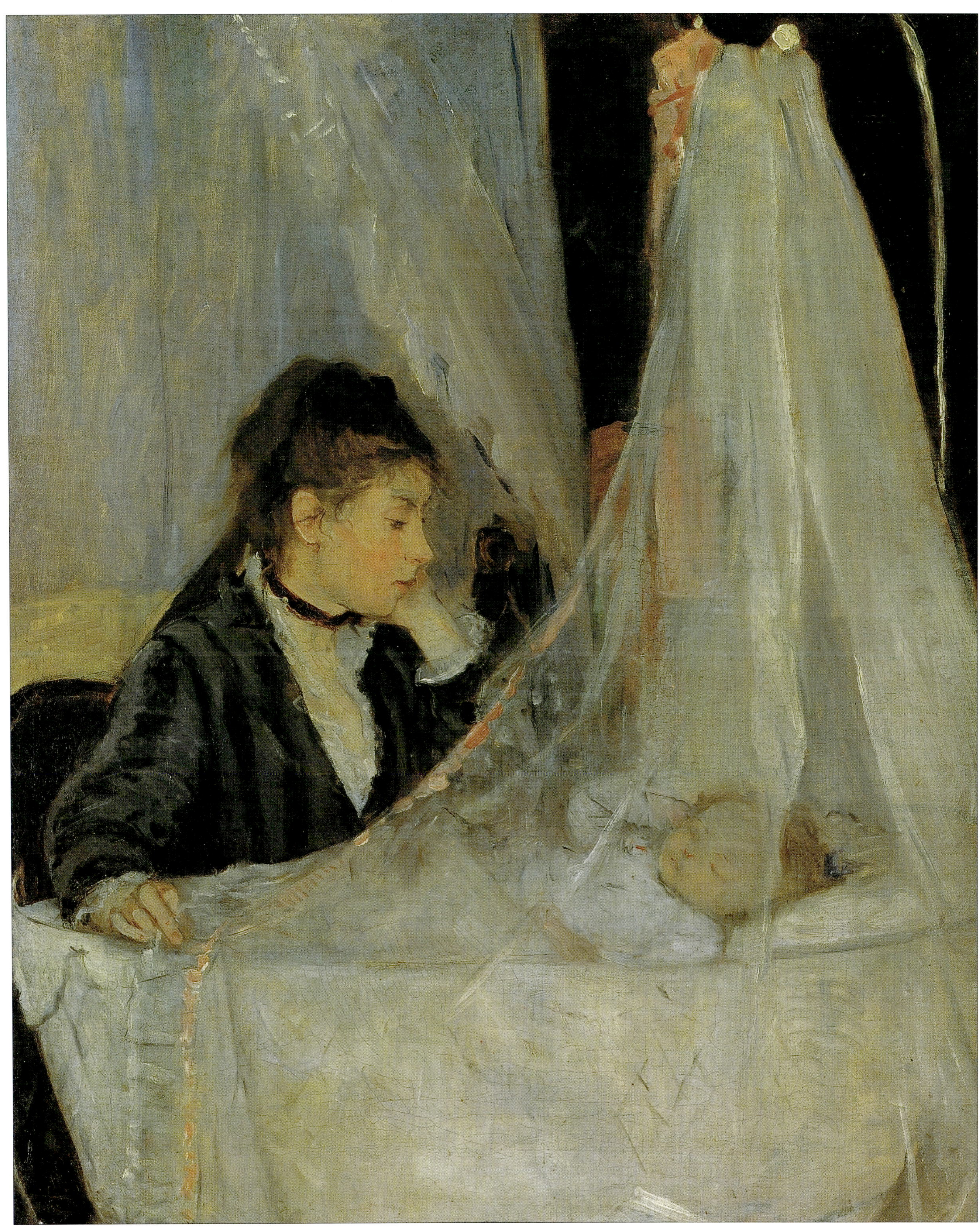

Pierre-Auguste Renoir

Madame Monet and Her Son

1874

Oil on canvas, 19⅞" × 26¾" (50.4 × 67.9cm). National Gallery of Art, Washington, D.C.

In July 1874, Renoir (1841–1919) went to stay with Monet and his family at Argenteuil, where he painted a series of portraits of Monet and his wife and child, and their fellow artist Alfred Sisley. Edouard Manet, who would also often visit the Monets, decided one day to sit side by side with Renoir as he painted a portrait of Camille and Jean in the garden. Dealing with a favorite Impressionist theme, the mother-and-child team enjoying a day of relaxation outdoors, Renoir has created an informal portrait which, despite its sketchy execution, retains an air of refined elegance and Parisian fashionability that is particularly visible in the woman's pose.

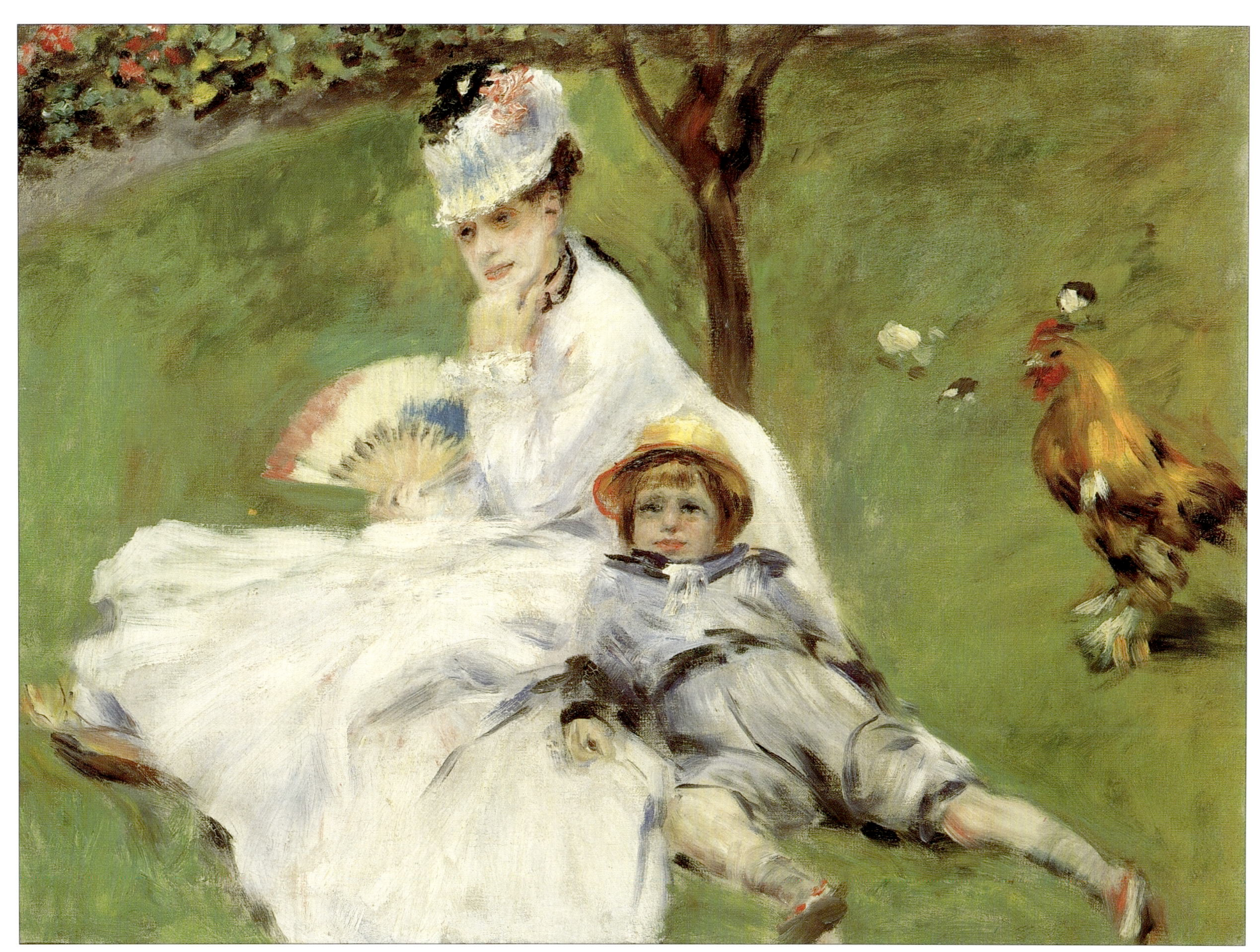

Mary Cassatt

Mother About to Wash Her Sleepy Child

1880

Oil on canvas, 39½" × 25¾" (100.3 × 65.4cm). Los Angeles County Museum of Art.

Born in Pittsburgh, Mary Cassatt (1844–1926) moved to Paris, where she joined the Impressionists. Like Morisot, she was financially independent and therefore able to pursue her career as a painter. Although she had no children, motherhood was a central theme of her work. In the fall of 1880, Cassatt's brother and his family came to Paris for a vacation. It was during this visit that Cassatt executed *Mother About to Wash Her Sleepy Child*, which is considered her first maternity image. Although Cassatt actually observed the daily routine of a woman washing her child, the pose of the baby with spread legs is in fact appropriated from one of Correggio's pictures of the Madonna and Child. The extended vertical format of the picture, further stressed by the wallpaper design and the stripes of the chair fabric, also points to the uplifting, transcendental format of much religious imagery. As in other works by Cassatt on the same theme, the two figures form a compact group, conveying a close and caring maternal relationship.

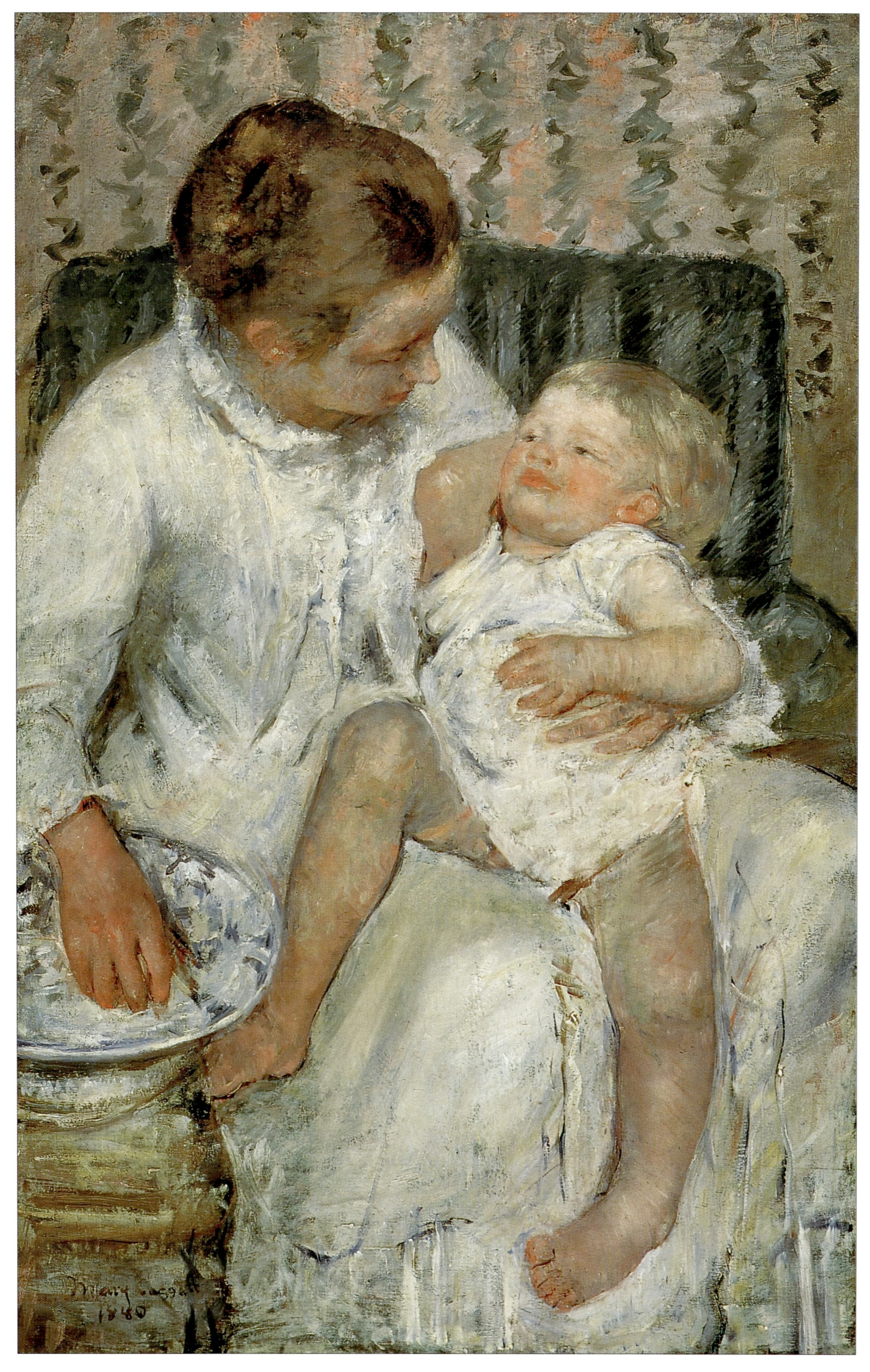

EUGÈNE CARRIÈRE

Winding Wool

(also called *The Spinners*)

1887

OIL ON CANVAS, 46" × 38" (116.8 × 96.5CM). TATE GALLERY, LONDON.

Carrière (1849–1906) is known for his scenes of motherhood and family life. *Winding Wool* conveys the emotional and physical bond between mother and daughter through this age-old domestic activity. Although Carrière used members of his own family as models, his figures rarely show strongly individual characteristics. His goal was to represent his family as archetypal of the family of all mankind. Accordingly, a generic rather than a specific portrayal of mother and child was essential to Carrière's approach. Obviously, the artist was interested in recording more than mere visual appearance. To him, bringing forth an image from the amorphous background was an act of spiritual dimension. His paintings tend to explore not the real world, but rather that of reverie, dream, and trance.

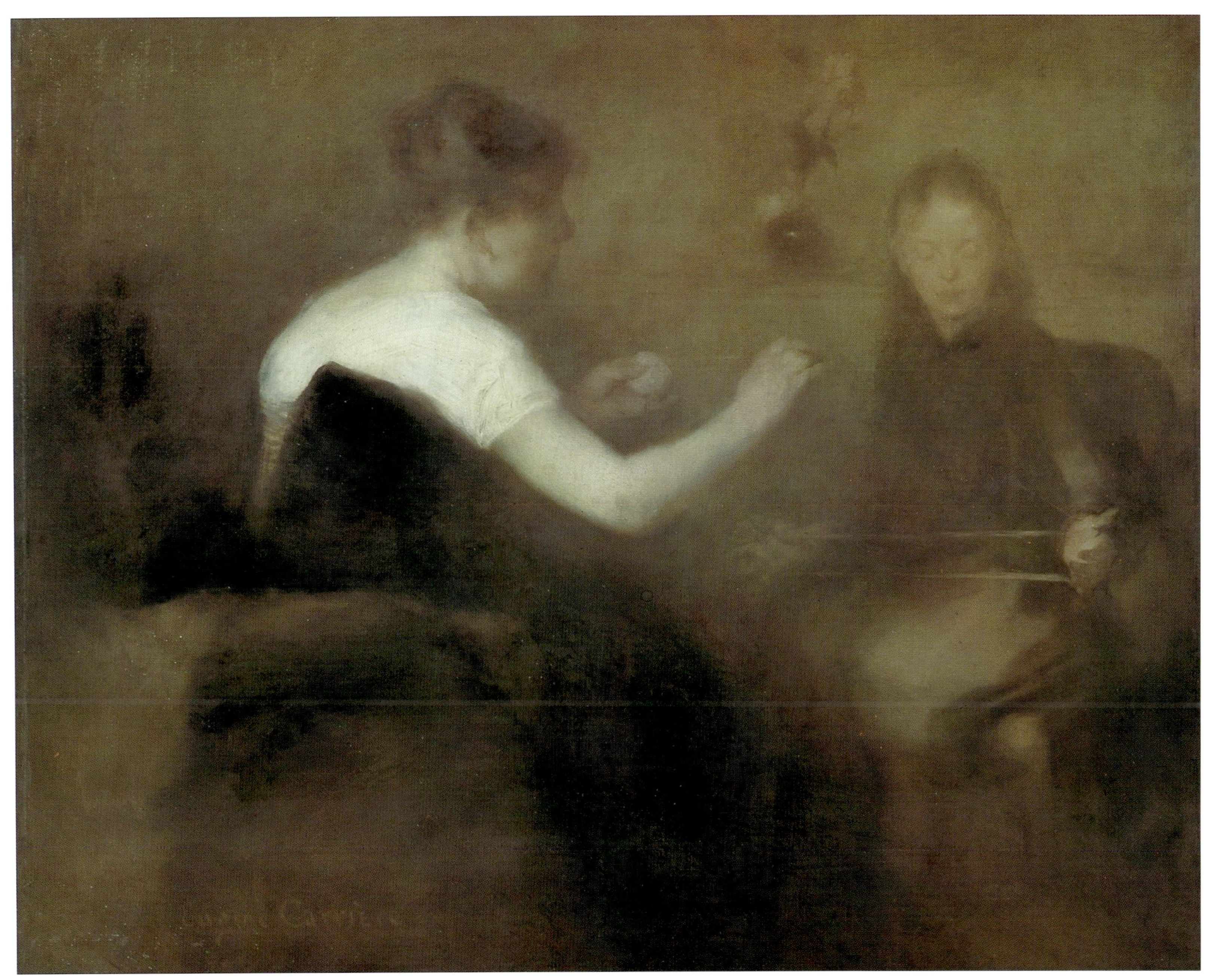

VINCENT VAN GOGH

Madame Roulin and Her Baby

1888–1889

OIL ON CANVAS, 36 3/8" × 28 7/8" (92.3 × 73.3CM). PHILADELPHIA MUSEUM OF ART.

In 1888, van Gogh (1853–1890) moved to Arles in the south of France, where he was to spend two years in a period of unsurpassed creativity. *Madame Roulin and Her Baby* belongs to a group of works van Gogh executed of the entire family of his very good friend from Arles, the postman Joseph Roulin. The portrait is of a four-month-old baby held in her mother's lap, and it was preceded by a similar work, now in the collection of the Metropolitan Museum of Art in New York City. Both paintings are proto-expressionistic in their strong and jagged contours, and in the anatomical distortions particularly visible in the depiction of the child. The two versions of *Madame Roulin and Her Baby* were followed by a major work, *La Berceuse*, another portrait of the postman's wife. In the latter work, the mother only suggests the presence of the baby by the gesture of holding the rope of the cradle she is rocking.

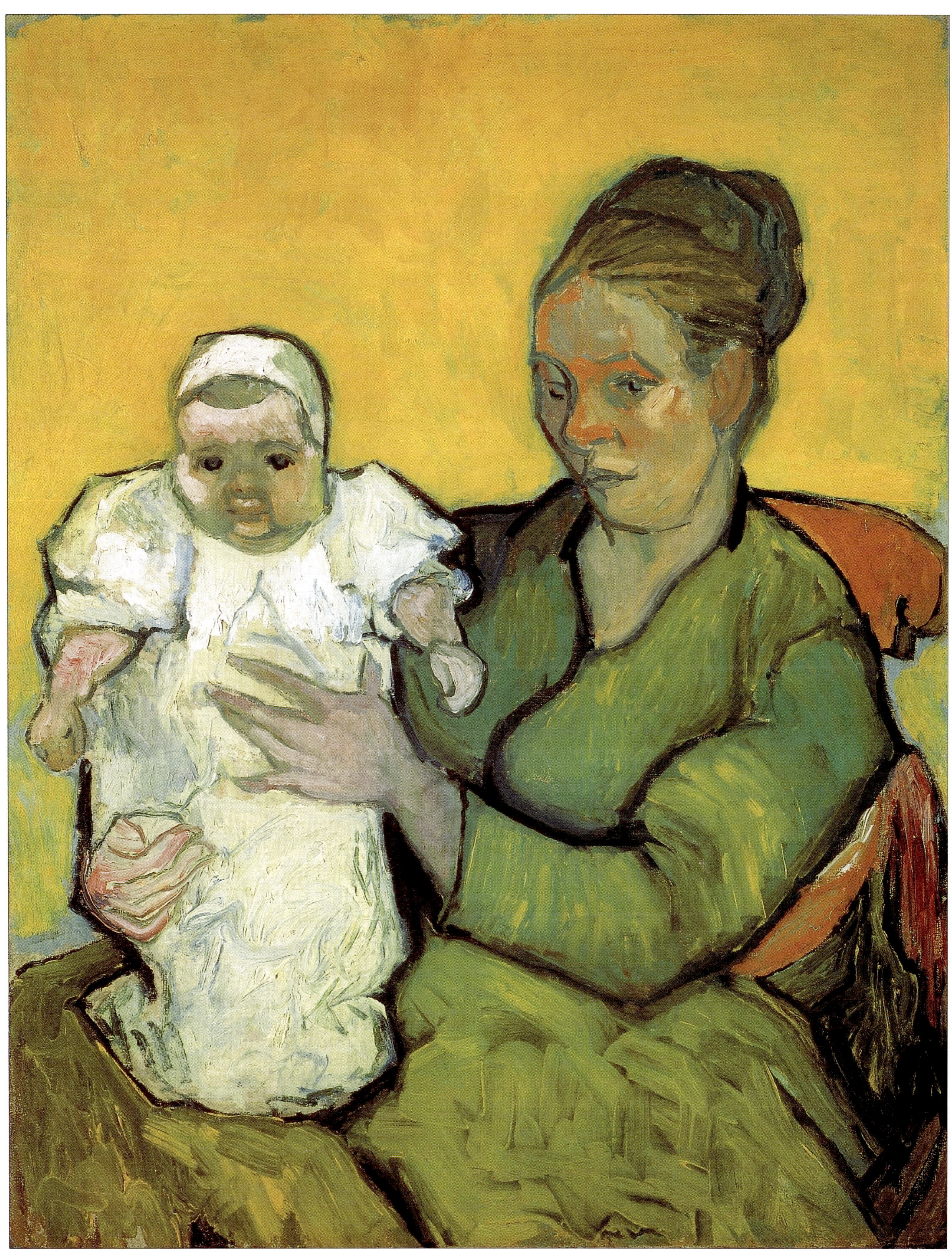

Eugène Carrière

Maternité

c. 1892

Oil on canvas, 37¾" × 45¾" (95.8 × 116.2cm). The Museum of Modern Art, New York.

Eugène Carrière's *Maternités* have often been interpreted as secularized images of the Old Masters' Madonnas. In fact, the paintings do share a quality of sacredness, arising from Carrière's belief that the relationship between mother and child symbolized the continuity and regeneration of all life. Carrière's use of vaporous and indistinct forms, renunciation of color with the exception of brown, and depiction of an undefinable space all point to an understanding of nature as ethereal and immaterial. The monochromatic washes and the softened focus are devices derived from Leonardo da Vinci's sfumato.

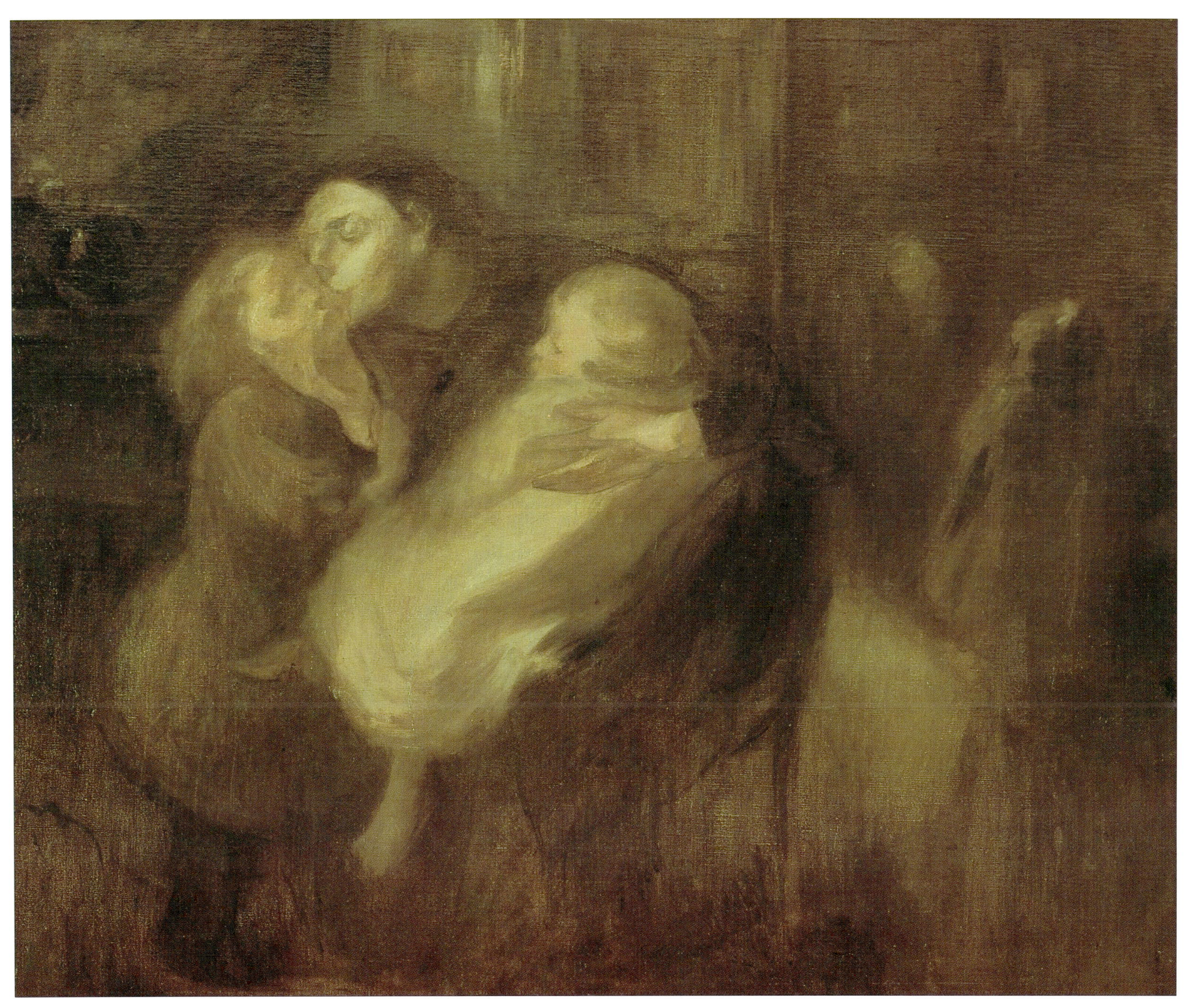

Mary Cassatt

Reine Lefebvre Holding a Nude Baby

1902

Oil on canvas, 26$\frac{3}{16}$" × 22$\frac{9}{16}$" (66.5 × 57.3cm). Worcester Art Museum, Massachusetts.

Mary Cassatt completed her first maternity painting in 1880. Having studied works on the same theme by Correggio, Parmigianino, and Rubens during her stay in Parma in the early 1870s, Cassatt chose to interpret motherhood in terms of a modern, secular Madonna. In this work the religious analogy is tempered by the fact that Reine Lefebvre's tight embrace with her nude baby was observed directly from life. Nevertheless, the adaptation of contemporary women into the Virgin and Child motif was an increasingly popular approach to the subject in nineteenth-century France. The two figures' interlocking pose reveals a relationship of mutual love, nurturing, and security.

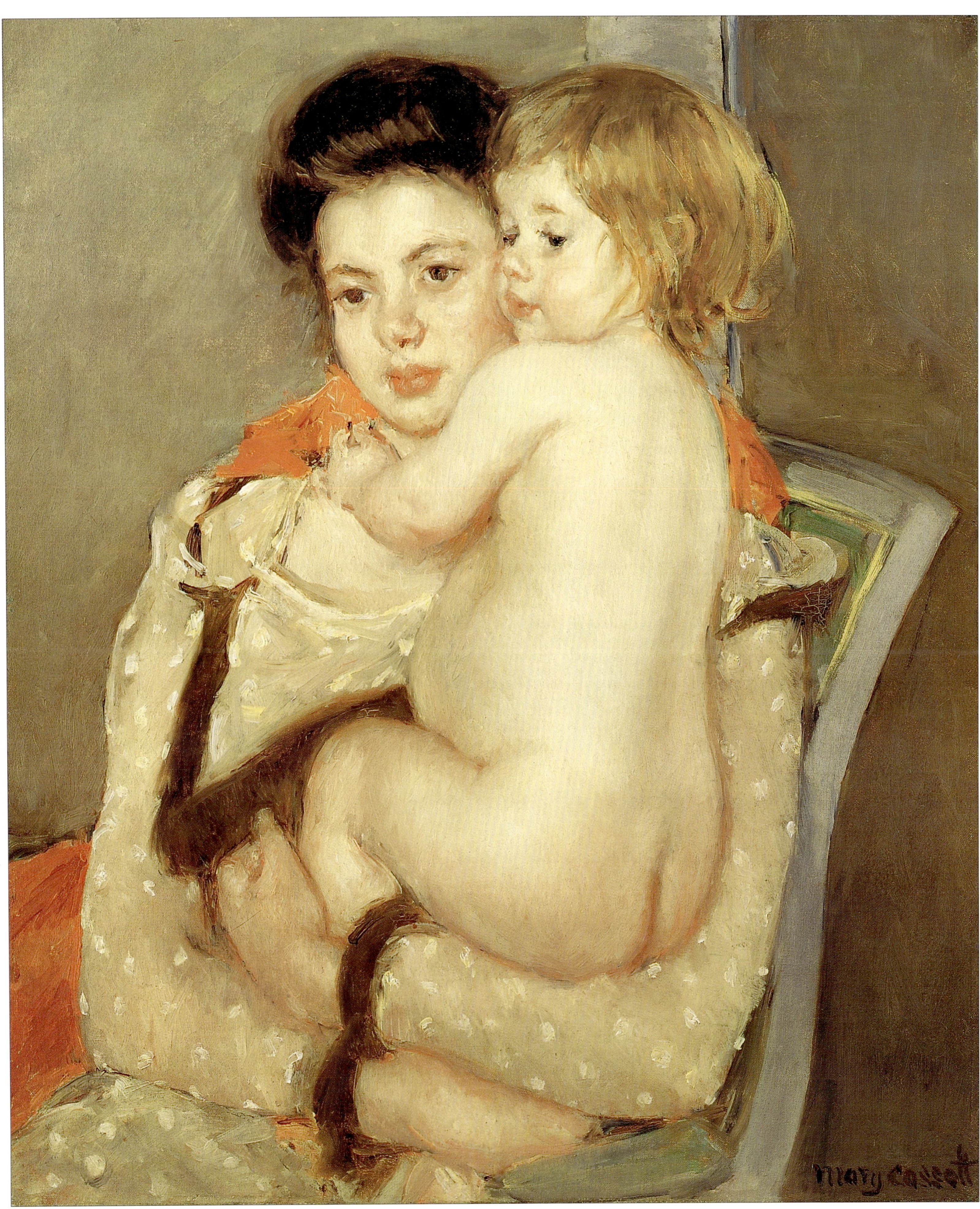
Mary Cassatt

Pablo Picasso

Mother and Child

1907

Oil on canvas, 31⅞" × 23⅝" (81 × 60cm). Musée Picasso, Paris.

Incredibly prolific, original, and versatile, Pablo Picasso (1881–1973) is without doubt one of the twentieth century's greatest artists. As one might expect, his treatment of the mother-and-child theme represents a daring departure from the approaches popular in the nineteenth century. *Mother and Child* (1907) was painted in a watershed year in Picasso's career. That year he visited the ethnographic museum at Palais du Trocadero and had a sudden "revelation" upon viewing African sculpture. Strongly influenced by the tribal art, Picasso experimented with greater abstraction of form, flat areas of color, and long striations or hatchings, conceiving the bold and primitivistic mother-and-child pair. More significant than any technical borrowings, however, is Picasso's ability to infuse the work with the same force he sensed in African sculpture—a power to stir intense emotions in the viewer.

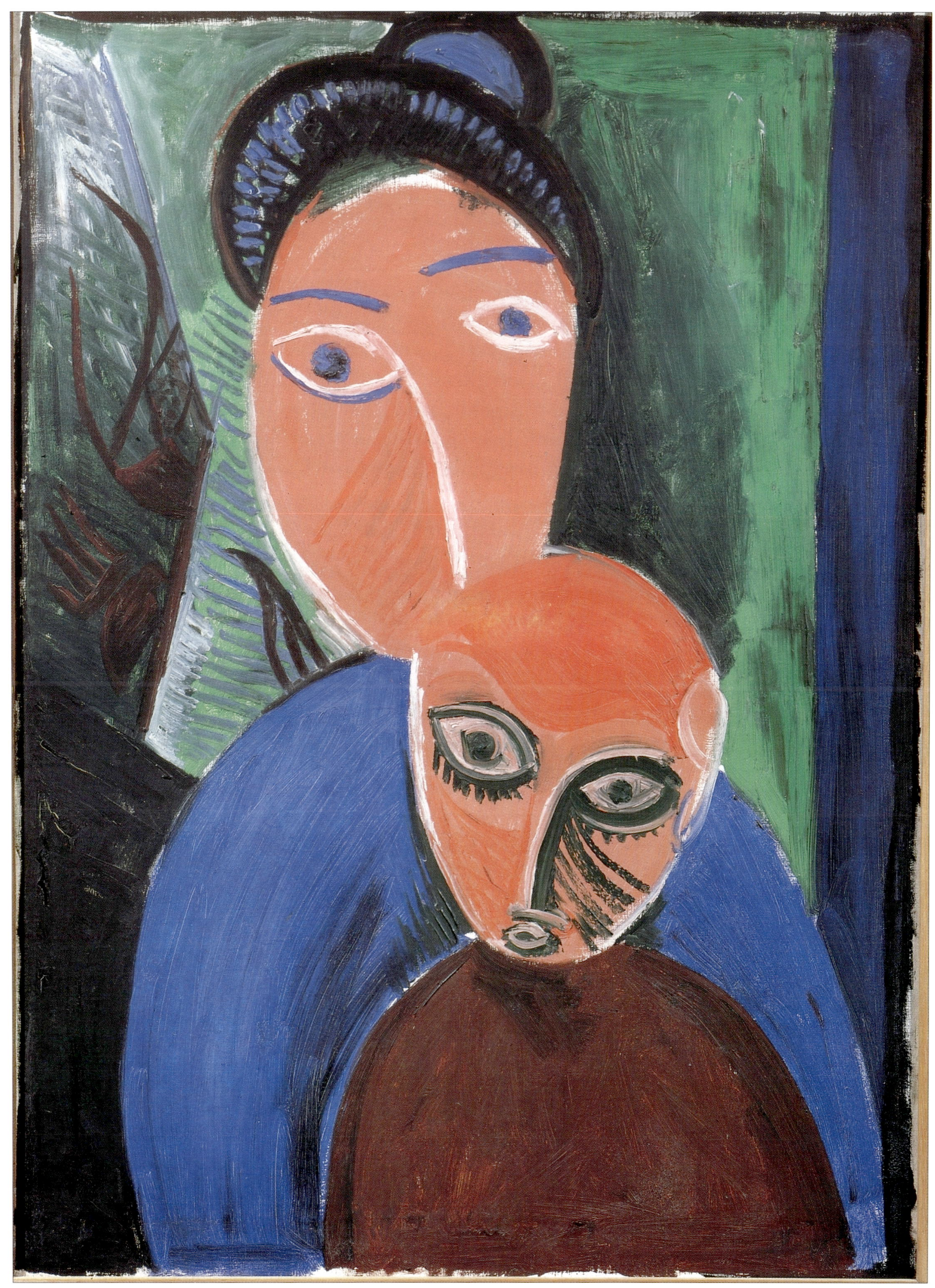

Pablo Picasso

Mother and Child

1921

Oil on canvas, 56 1/2" × 64" (143.5 × 162.5cm). The Art Institute of Chicago.

The early 1920s comprised Picasso's Neoclassical period, during which he was inspired by the monumental forms of Greek and Roman antiquity. On February 4, 1921, his wife Olga gave birth to a boy, an event that prompted Picasso to create *Mother and Child*. In this work, Picasso used anatomical distortions and large size to make a psychological point. The mammoth figure is a representation of the mother as perceived by the child: larger than life, protective, powerful. Differently put, the child understands the world via his mother, and the mother is the embodiment of the world. The woman is thus a modern-day fertility symbol, the Great Mother, a life-giving force.

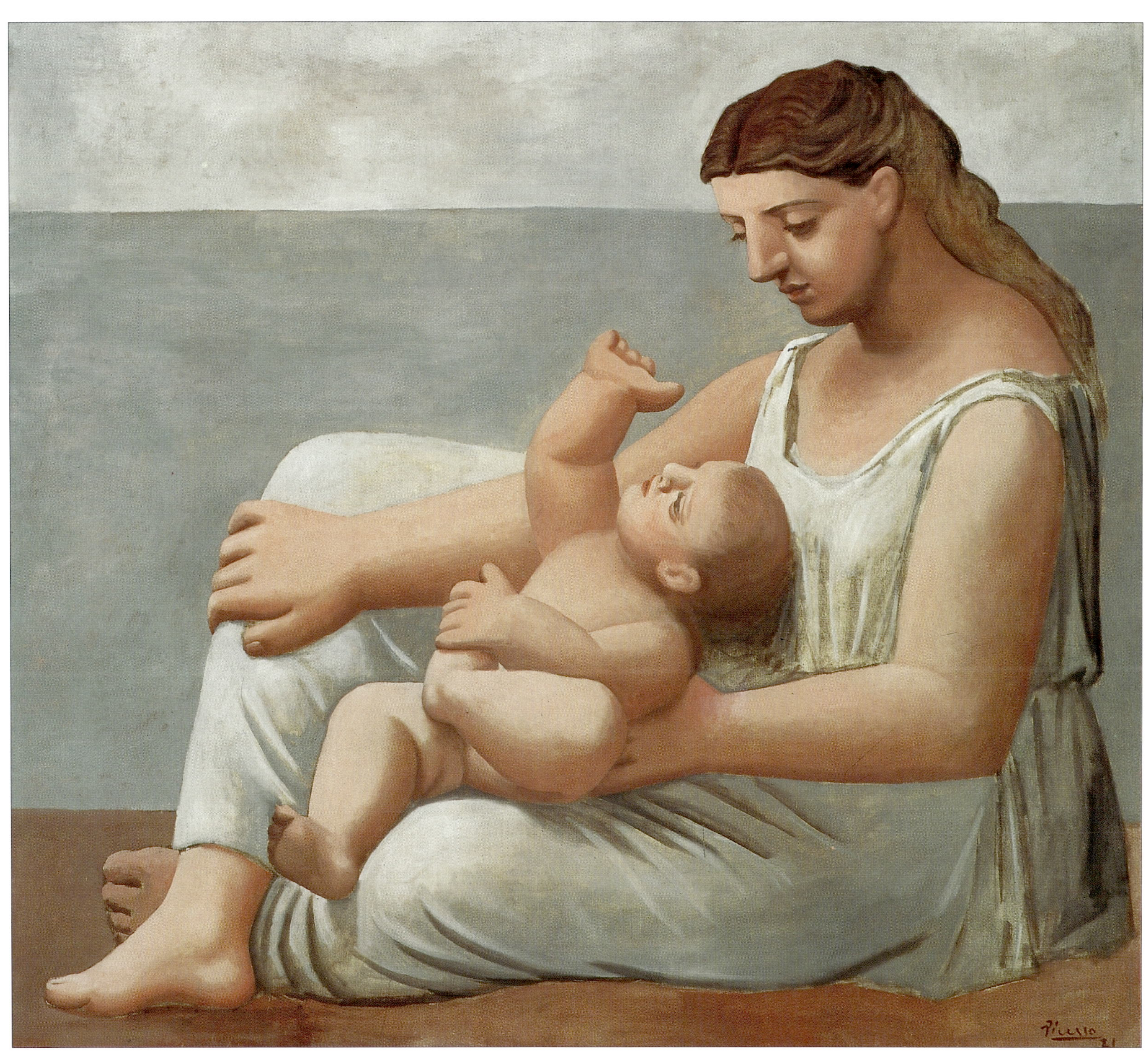

Joan Miró

Maternity

1924

Oil on canvas, 35 7/8" × 29 1/8" (91.1 × 74cm). Scottish National Gallery of Modern Art, Edinburgh.

In 1924 Joan Miró (1893–1983) began taking an active part in the Surrealist movement, and on that occasion André Breton declared him "the most 'surrealist' of us all." Stimulated by the Surrealist concept of creating work that is a pure reflection of the subconscious, Miró produced abstract works that featured fluid shapes and delicate lines. *Maternity* is a work of singular interest insofar as it marks a further step in Miró's use of cryptic signs. It is more sparse and is purged of the diversity of details characteristic of Miró's earlier paintings. Here the elements are used with strict economy and placed in an almost organic relationship with each other. The work is closely linked to *The Family* (1924), in which the head of the mother figure is represented by a simple black shape crowned with hair radiating from it. In *Maternity*, the movement of the two insectlike forms toward the breastlike shapes indicate in abstract idiom the primal oral attachment of child and mother.

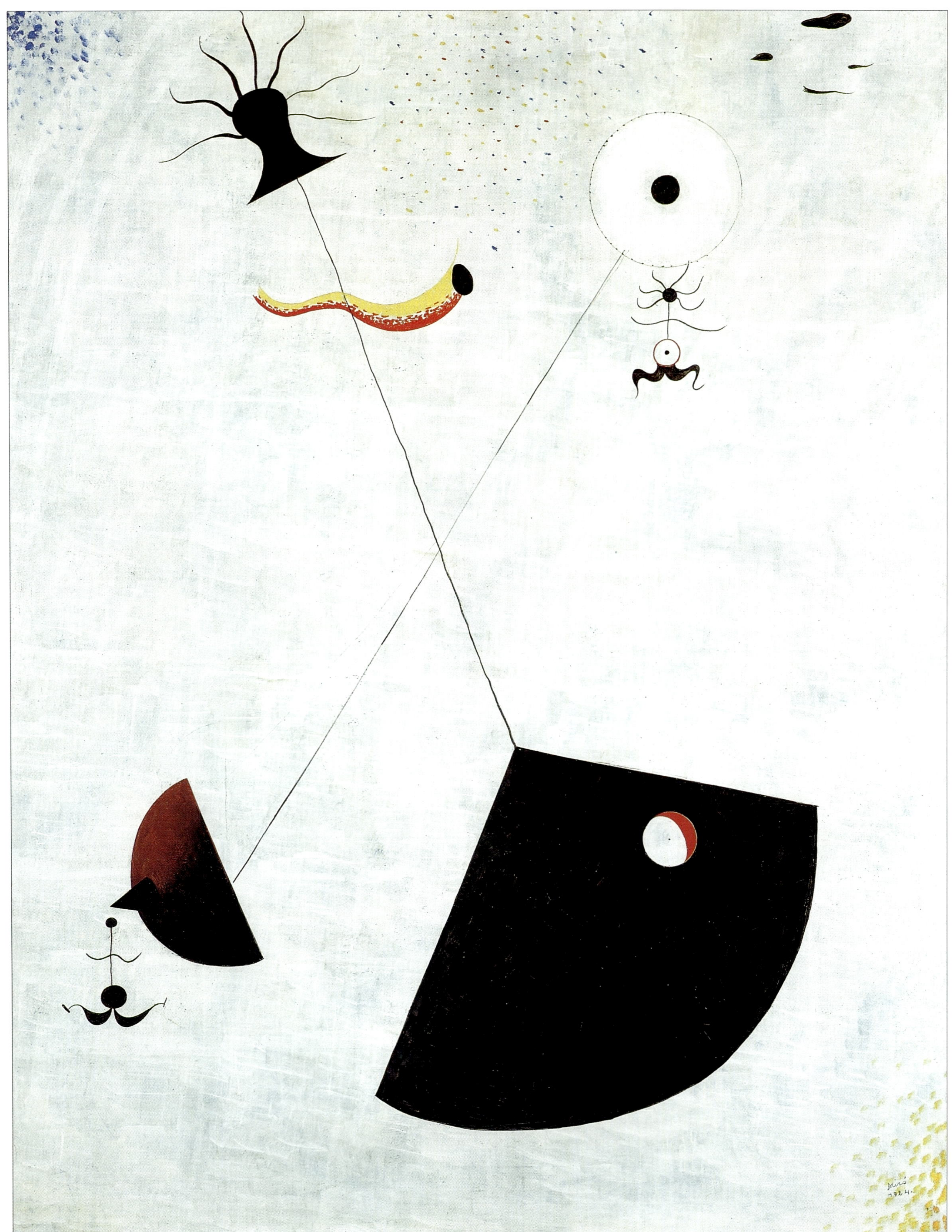
Miró
1924.

Arshile Gorky

The Artist and His Mother

c. 1926–1936

Oil on canvas, 60" × 50" (152.4 × 127cm). Whitney Museum of American Art, New York.

Before coming to be known as an important painter of the Abstract Expressionist school, Gorky (1904–1948) produced his most famous early work, a self-portrait with his mother. Based on a melancholy photograph taken in 1912 in Armenia when Gorky was only eight, the picture preoccupied the artist from the mid-1920s through the mid-1930s. Working on it intermittently for a full decade, Gorky generated many preparatory drawings and paintings in various stages of completion. The version housed at the Whitney Museum is probably the most finished treatment. The autobiographical scene translates the medieval devotional theme of an acolyte standing beside the Madonna into modern terms. Influenced by a double legacy—the portraiture of Cézanne and the synthetic Cubism of Picasso—the work merges stylistic experimentation with a deeply felt personal sentiment.

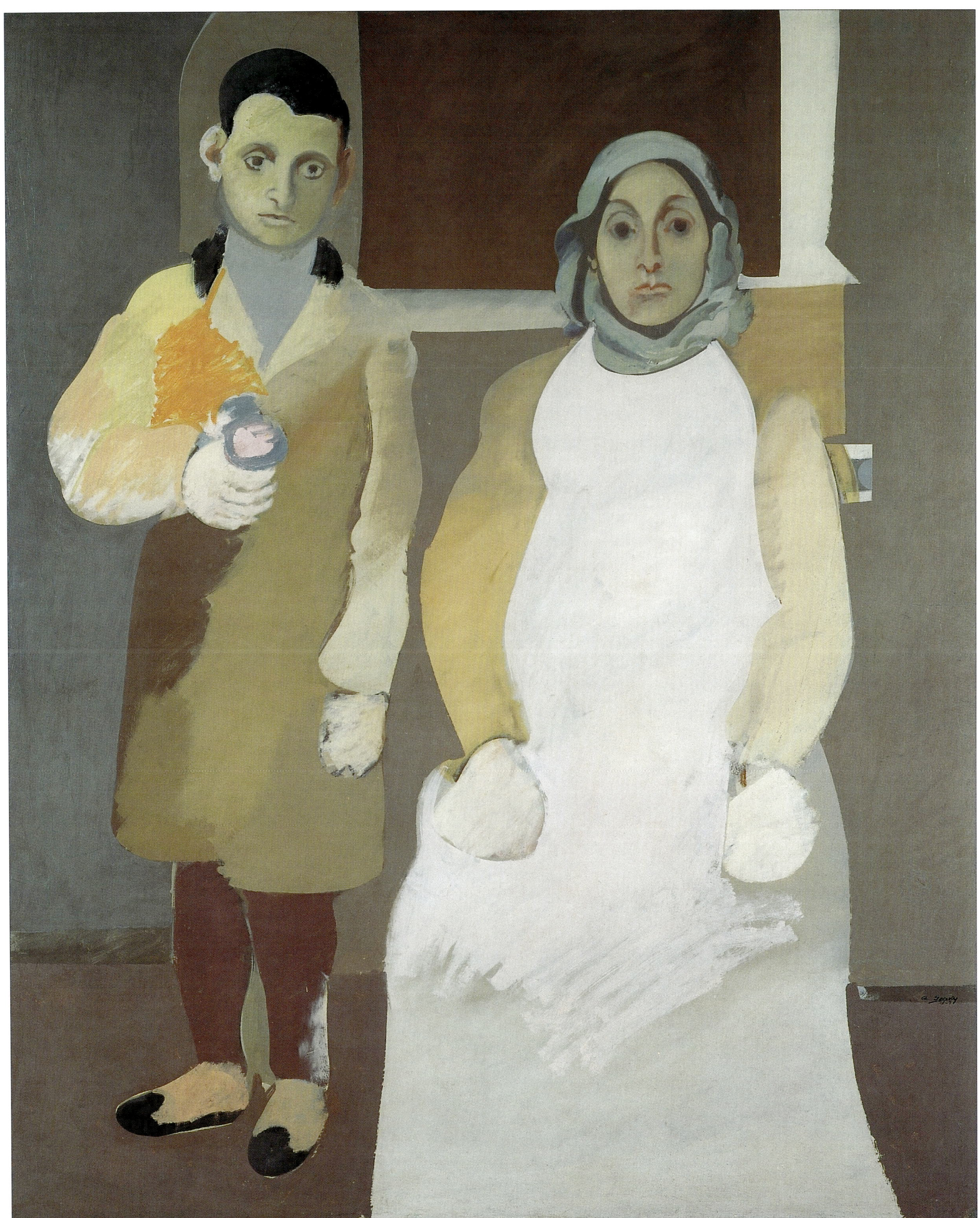

PABLO PICASSO

First Steps

1943

OIL ON CANVAS, 51¼" × 38¼" (130.1 × 97.1CM). YALE UNIVERSITY ART GALLERY, NEW HAVEN, CONNECTICUT.

First Steps is a family portrait of Picasso's housekeeper Ines, who worked at Hôtel Vaste Horizon in Mougin where the artist used to spend his summers, and her baby daughter. The anatomical depiction of the two figures is willfully distorted, as is the use of the double-faced motif that Picasso favored at the time. The child's face in particular presents a profile, yet with both eyes, ears, and nostrils fully visible. The combination of Cubist-derived fragmentation, Neoclassical monumentality, and caricature within a single work points to Picasso's unique hybrid of versatility, humor, and stylistic innovation.

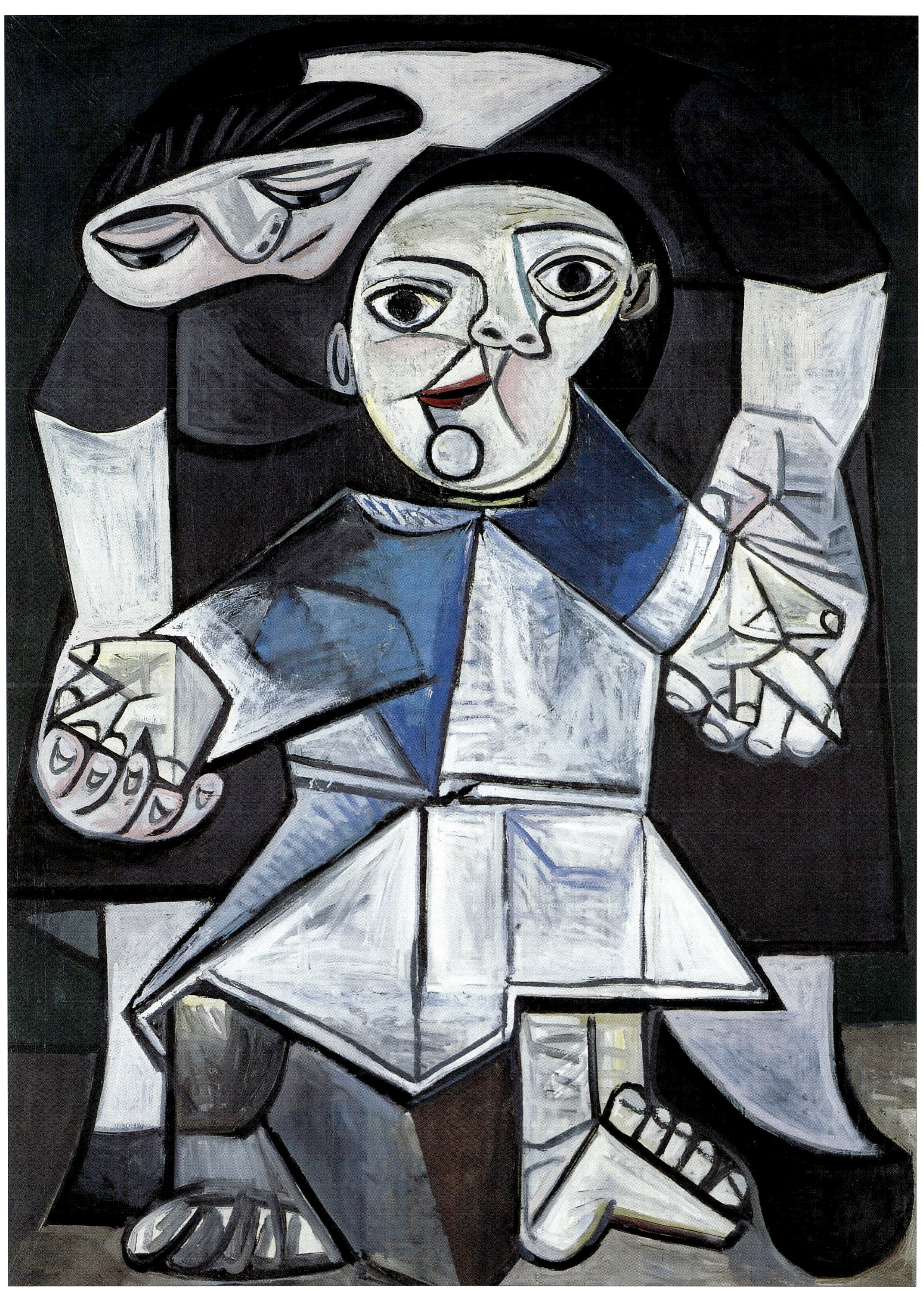

Salvador Dali

Madonna of Port Lligat

1949

Oil on canvas, 19½" × 15$^{1}/_{16}$" (49.5 × 38.2cm).
Patrick and Beatrice Haggerty Museum of Art, Marquette University, Milwaukee.

Dali (1904–1989) developed a type of Freudian Surrealism that featured recurring images, including classical references and esoteric allusions to Catalonia. *Madonna of Port Lligat* is Dali's first large work on a religious theme. The model for the Madonna was the artist's wife, Gala, while the son of a local fisherman posed for the Christ Child. The Madonna is sublimated in a tabernacle in the center of which the Infant, with a tabernacle cut into his chest, holds a piece of the Eucharist bread. In his 1950 version of *Madonna of Port Lligat*, Dali incorporated a rhinoceros horn, which is a reference to both the mythical white unicorn, a symbol of the Madonna's chastity, and the history of Port Lligat. Dali's paintings derive much of their power from his use of realistic detail in unreal, settings, complete with carefully depicted, strangely hallucinatory imagery. His style has been called Magic Realism.

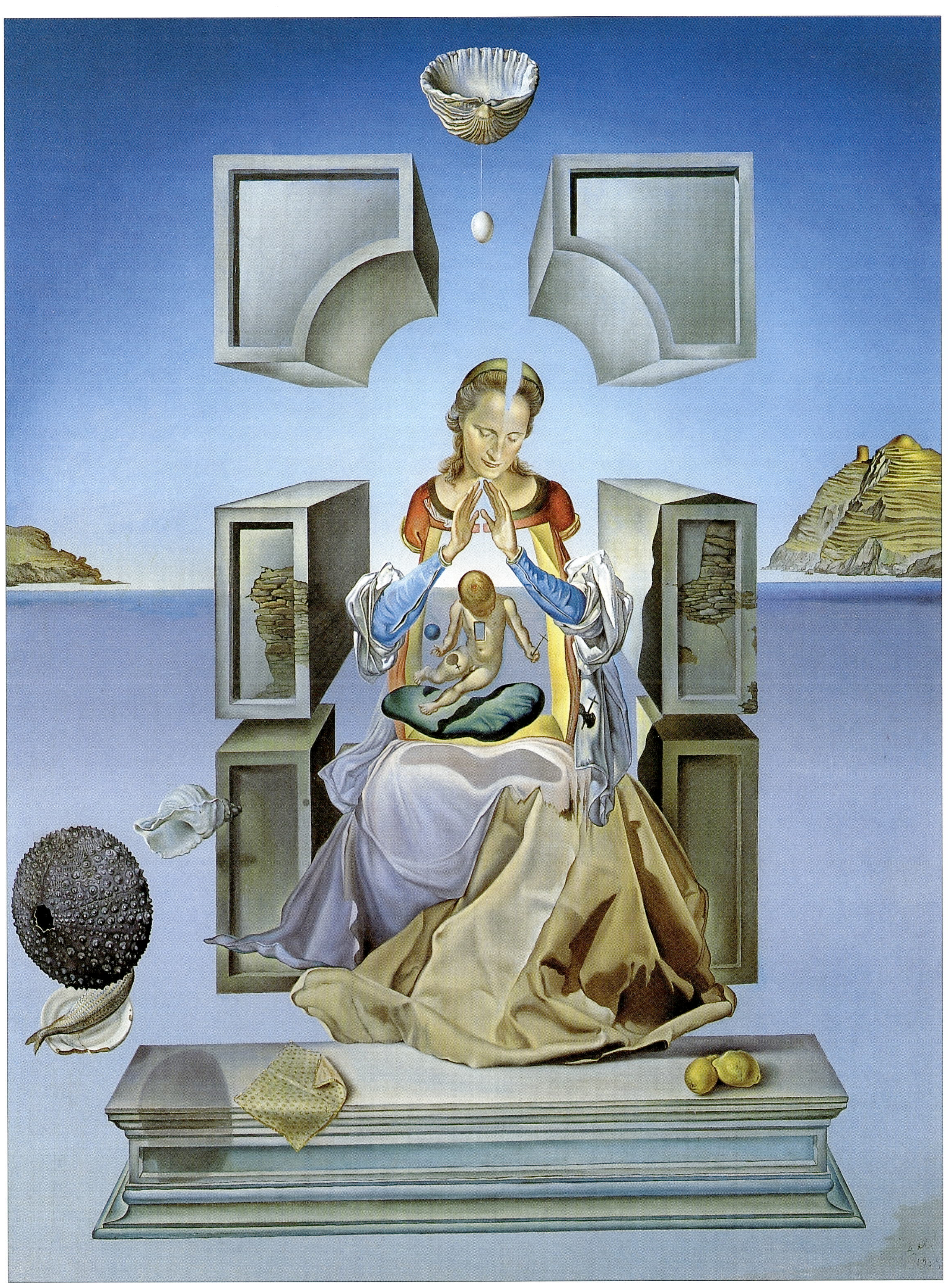

Photography Credits

Pablo Picasso, Spanish (1881–1973), *Mother and Child*, 1921, oil on canvas, 56½" × 64" (143.5 × 162.5cm), Gift of Maymar Corporation, Mrs. Maurice L. Rothschild, Mr. and Mrs. Chauncey McCormick; Mary and Leigh Block Charitable Fund; Ada Turnbull Hertle Endowment; through prior gift of Mr. and Mrs. Edwin E. Hokin, 1954.270, photograph © 1993, The Art Institute of Chicago, All Rights Reserved.

Mary Cassatt, American (1844–1926), *The Bath*, 1891–1892, oil on canvas, 39½" × 26" (100.3 × 66cm), Photograph © 1994, The Art Institute of Chicago, All rights reserved, Robert A. Waller Fund, 1910.2

Parmigianino (Francesco Mazzola), *Madonna of the Long Neck*, 1534–1540, oil on wood, 85" × 52" (216 × 132cm), Galleria degli Uffizi, Florence, Erich Lessing/Art Resource, NY

Marguerite Gérard (1761–1837), *Sleep My Child*, c. 1783–1785, oil on canvas, 21⅝" × 17¾" (55 × 45cm), Staatliche Kunsthalle Karlsruhe

Giotto di Bondone, *Madonna and Child Enthroned*, c. 1310, oil on panel, 128" × 80¼" (325.1 × 203.8cm), Galleria degli Uffizi, Florence, Scala/Art Resource, NY

Fra Filippo Lippi, *Madonna and Child (Tarquinia Madonna)*, 1437, oil on panel, 45" × 25½" (114.3 × 64.7cm), Galleria Nazionale d'Arte Antica, Rome, Scala/Art Resource, NY

Hans Memling, Bruges (active c. 1465–1494), *Madonna and Child with Angels*, after 1479, oil on panel, painted surface: 22⅝" × 18¼" (57.6 × 46.4cm); panel: 23⅛" × 18⅞" (58.8 × 48cm); framed: 34" × 30½" × 4½" (86.3 × 77.4 × 11.4cm), Andrew W. Mellon Collection, © 1994 Board of Trustees, National Gallery of Art, Washington

Leonardo da Vinci, *Madonna and St. Anne*, c. 1501–1513, oil on panel, 66¼" × 51¼" (168.2 × 130.1cm), Musée du Louvre, Paris, Scala/Art Resource, NY

Raphael, *Madonna of the Meadows*, 1505, oil on panel, 45" × 25½" (114.3 × 64.7cm), Kunsthistorisches Museum, Vienna, Erich Lessing/Art Resource, NY

Albrecht Dürer, *Madonna with the Slice of Pear*, 1512, oil on pinewood, 19¼" × 14⅝" (60.3 × 37.1cm), Kunsthistorisches Museum, Vienna, Erich Lessing/Art Resource, NY

Titian, *Madonna with a Rabbit* (also called *Madonna and Child with St. Catherine of Alexandria and a Shepherd*), c. 1529–1530, oil on canvas, 33" × 27½" (84 × 70cm), Musée du Louvre, Paris, Giraudon/Art Resource, NY

Agnolo Bronzino, *Portrait of Eleonora of Toledo with Her Son Giovanni*, 1550, oil on panel, 45¼" × 37¾" (114.9 × 95.8cm), Galleria degli Uffizi, Florence, Scala/Art Resource, NY

Pieter de Hooch, Dutch (1629–1684), *Woman Nursing an Infant with a Child Feeding a Dog*, c. 1658–1660, oil on canvas, 26⅝" × 21¹³⁄₁₆" (67.6 × 55.4cm), The Fine Arts Museums of San Francisco, Gift of the Samuel H. Kress Foundation

Gerard Ter Borch, *Woman Peeling Apples*, c. 1660, oil on canvas, attached to panel, 14⅛" × 12" (35.8 × 30.4cm), Kunsthistorisches Museum, Vienna

Jean-Baptiste Siméon Chardin, *Saying Grace*, 1740, oil on canvas, 19½" × 15⅛" (49.5 × 38.5cm), Musée du Louvre, Paris, Giraudon/Art Resource, NY

Sir Joshua Reynolds, *Lady Cockburn and Her Three Eldest Sons*, 1773, oil on canvas, 55¾" × 44½" (141.6 × 113cm), The National Gallery, London

Angelica Kauffmann, born Swiss (1741–1807), *Cornelia Pointing to Her Children as Her Treasures*, c. 1785, oil on canvas, 40" × 50" (101.6 × 127cm), Virginia Museum of Fine Arts, Richmond, The Adolph D. and Wilkins C. Williams Fund

Marie-Louise-Élisabeth Vigée-Lebrun, *Marie-Antoinette and Her Children*, 1787, oil on canvas, 104" × 82" (264.1 × 208.2cm), Musée National du Château de Versailles et de Trianon, Giraudon/Art Resource, NY

Ford Madox Brown, *Pretty Baa-Lambs*, 1851–1859, oil on panel, 24" × 30" (60.9 × 76.2cm), published by permission of the Birmingham Museum and Art Gallery

Claude Monet (1840–1926), *The Luncheon*, 1868, oil on canvas, 90½" × 59" (230 × 150cm), Städelsches Kunstinstitut und Städtische Galerie, Frankfurt, Artothek

Claude Monet (1840–1926), *Wild Poppies*, 1873, oil on canvas, 19¾" × 25½" (50.1 × 64.7cm), Musée d'Orsay, Paris, Erich Lessing/Art Resource, NY

Berthe Morisot, *Catching Butterflies*, 1873, oil on canvas, 18" × 22" (45.7 × 55.8cm), Musée d'Orsay, Paris, Giraudon/Art Resource, NY

Berthe Morisot, *The Cradle*, 1873, oil on canvas, 22½" × 18½" (57.1 × 47cm), Musée d'Orsay, Paris, Erich Lessing/Art Resource, NY

Pierre-Auguste Renoir, French (1841–1919), *Madame Monet and Her Son*, 1874, oil on canvas, 19⅞" × 26¾" (50.4 × 67.9cm); framed: 30½" × 37⅝" × 4½" (77.4 × 95.5 × 11.4cm), National Gallery of Art, Washington, D.C., Ailsa Mellon Bruce Collection

Mary Cassatt, United States (1844–1926), *Mother About to Wash Her Sleepy Child*, 1880, oil on canvas, 39½" × 25¾" (100.3 × 65.4cm), Los Angeles County Museum of Art, Mrs. Fred Hathaway Bixby Bequest

Eugène Carrière, *Winding Wool* (also called *The Spinners*), 1887, oil on canvas, 46" × 38" (116.8 × 96.5cm), Tate Gallery, London/Art Resource, NY

Vincent van Gogh, Dutch (1853–1890), *Madame Roulin and Her Baby*, 1888–1889, oil on canvas, 36⅜" × 28⅞" (92.3 × 73.3cm), Philadelphia Museum of Art, Bequest of Lisa Norris Elkins

Eugène Carrière, *Maternité*, c. 1892, oil on canvas, 37¾" × 45¾" (95.8 × 116.2cm), The Museum of Modern Art, New York. Given anonymously. Photograph © 1994 The Museum of Modern Art, New York

Mary Cassatt, United States (1844–1926), *Reine Lefebvre Holding a Nude Baby*, 1902, oil on canvas, 26³⁄₁₆" × 22⁹⁄₁₆" (66.5 × 57.3cm), Worcester Art Museum, Worcester, Massachusetts

Pablo Picasso, Spanish (1881–1973), *Mother and Child*, 1907, oil on canvas, 31⅞" × 23⅝" (81 × 60cm), Musée Picasso, Paris, © ARS, NY, Giraudon/Art Resource, NY

Joan Miro, *Maternity*, 1924, oil on canvas, 35⅞" × 29⅛" (91.1 × 74cm), Scottish National Gallery of Modern Art, Edinburgh

Arshile Gorky (1904–1948), *The Artist and His Mother*, c. 1926–1936, oil on canvas, 60" × 50" (152.4 × 127cm), Collection of Whitney Museum of American Art, New York, Gift of Julien Levy for Maro and Natasha Gorky in memory of their father, 50.17

Pablo Picasso, Spanish (1881–1973), *First Steps*, 1943, oil on canvas, 51¼" × 38¼" (130.1 × 97.1cm), Yale University Art Gallery, New Haven, CT, Gift of Stephen C. Clark, B.A. 1903

Salvador Dali, Spanish (1904–1989), *Madonna of Port Lligat*, 1949, oil on canvas, 19½" × 15¹⁄₁₆" (49.5 × 38.2cm), Patrick and Beatrice Haggerty Museum of Art, Marquette University, Milwaukee, WI, Gift of Mr. and Mrs. Ira Haupt, 59.9, © 1994 Marquette University. All rights reserved. No part of this transparency may be reproduced without the permission of The Patrick and Beatrice Haggerty Museum of Art, Marquette University, Milwaukee, WI 53233, USA